The Paradox of Connection

The Paradox of Connection

How Digital Media Is
Transforming Journalistic Labor

DIANA BOSSIO, VALÉRIE BÉLAIR-GAGNON,
AVERY E. HOLTON, AND LOGAN MOLYNEUX

UNIVERSITY OF
ILLINOIS PRESS
Urbana, Chicago, and Springfield

Library of Congress Cataloging-in-Publication Data

Names: Bossio, Diana, 1980– author. | Bélair-Gagnon, Valérie,
    author. | Holton, Avery, author. | Molyneux, Logan, author.
Title: The paradox of connection : how digital media is
    transforming journalistic labor / Diana Bossio, Valérie Bélair-
    Gagnon, Avery Holton, and Logan Molyneux.
Description: Urbana : University of Illinois Press, 2024. | Includes
    bibliographical references and index.
Identifiers: LCCN 2023024563 (print) | LCCN 2023024564
    (ebook) | ISBN 9780252045615 (cloth) | ISBN
    9780252087738 (paperback) | ISBN 9780252055270 (ebook)
Subjects: LCSH: Social media and journalism. | Online
    journalism. | Journalism—Technological innovations. |
    Misinformation. | Digital media.
Classification: LCC PN4766 .B67 2024 (print) | LCC PN4766
    (ebook) | DDC 302.23—dc23/eng/20231106
LC record available at https://lccn.loc.gov/2023024563
LC ebook record available at https://lccn.loc.gov/2023024564

Dedicated to journalists facing harassment, intimidation,
or violence for bringing news to the public.

Contents

Acknowledgments

We are grateful to those who helped us develop this book, especially the journalists, managers, and media workers we have been talking to and whose work we have been observing for more than a decade. We are also indebted to Nick Manolis, a doctoral student at Temple University's Klein College of Media and Communication. Nick provided insightful comments on each chapter and assisted with references and indexing. We also want to thank Colin Agur, Kath Albury, Kenzie Burchell, Matt Carlson, David Cheruyiot, Elisia Cohen, Raul Ferrer Conill, Letrell Crittenden, Mark Deuze, Stephanie Fielding, Lucas Graves, Antoine Haywood, Bente Kalsnes, Seth C. Lewis, Claudia Mellado, Jacob L. Nelson, Henrik Örnebring, Zizi Papacharissi, Robert Picard, Sue Robinson, Steen Steensen, Benjamin Toff, Nikki Usher, J. Siguru Wahutu, Andrea Wenzel, Oscar Westlund, and the OsloMet Digital Journalism Research Group (DJRG) for their insightful comments and suggestions and, as always, wonderful informal research conversations.

Diana would like to acknowledge the assistance of the Department of Media and Communication at Swinburne University for research time. Valérie would like to thank the Hubbard School of Journalism and Mass Communication and the College of Liberal Arts at the University of Minnesota for support of the project. She would also like to thank her accountability writing group (including Aynne Kokas, Allison Novak, Jen Shadie, and Josh Braun) for their help and insight into this project. Logan is grateful for research support from

Temple University, including providing a research assistant and summer research funding tied to this project. Avery is thankful to the University of Utah and the Department of Communication and the university's Communication Institute for their research support. He is additionally grateful to Sherwin Chua and the University of Gothenburg's Department of Journalism, Media and Communication for their global research support and engagement around many of the issues presented in this book.

We acknowledge that our universities are located on the traditional lands of Indigenous people. Diana would like to acknowledge that she wrote parts of this book on the unceded lands of the Boon Wurrung and Wurundjeri people of the Kulin Nation. Valérie wrote part of this book at the University of Minnesota–Twin Cities, which is located on traditional, ancestral, and contemporary lands of Indigenous people. The university resides on Dakota land ceded in the Treaties of 1837 and 1851. Avery worked on this book from the University of Utah and space that is named for the Ute Tribe. This land is the traditional and ancestral homeland of the Shoshone, Paiute, Goshute, and Ute Tribes and is a crossroad of the Indigenous peoples of Utah. Logan worked on this book in the Philadelphia area, land that originally belonged to the Lenape people. We pay respect to the traditional custodians of the lands on which this book was written and their elders past and present.

We also thank Daniel M. Nasset at the University of Illinois Press, who believed in this book and helped us shepherd it to the end. We are also grateful to the three anonymous peer reviewers for their insight and to the copyeditor. Finally, we are thankful and indebted to our families, friends, and colleagues who supported us in completing this project during a global pandemic and political and environmental turmoil.

Introduction

When Maria Ressa discovered she had won the Nobel Peace Prize for Journalism in late 2021, she was in the midst of fighting jail time. The Filipino American journalist and founder of the Manila-based online news site *Rappler* was appealing a six-year prison sentence for a libel conviction, one of several lawsuits seeking to criminalize her work in the Philippines. *Rappler* connects global audiences to investigative journalism about mass killings within corrupt police campaigns masterminded by Philippines president Rodrigo Duterte. But as Ressa's online support and engagement grew, so too did attacks from supporters of President Duterte. Political actors amplified online trolling and harassment to the extent that Ressa feared for her safety both online and offline.[1] Ressa said the online abuse was constant: "There were so many hate messages. Ninety hate messages an hour, 90 rape threats per minute. When I was younger, I was a war correspondent. That was easier than this."[2] It is here that journalists like Ressa reveal the paradox of online connection: for all the opportunities social media brings to journalists, there has been a corresponding rise in its harms, including escalating online harassment, reputational damage, and partisan reportage.[3]

The promise of connection centers on the myriad ways journalists can now engage with audiences, foster discussion, and create ever faster, ever cheaper, and ever more accessible forms of making and distributing news. Journalists and news organizations have distinguished themselves through the innovative use of social media tools. For example, the development of collaborative data journalism after the release of the Panama Papers has allowed convictions for tax evasion by the superrich totaling $1.2 billion so far. Global journalists worked alongside Egyptian activists to use Twitter and mobile phones to produce award-winning reporting on the Arab Spring.[4] These efforts raised hopes for development of more transparent, interconnected, collaborative, and participatory journalism.[5]

The reality has been much more complicated.

The idea for this book emerged when we each noticed a growing problem in professional journalism. Our research increasingly identified journalists who were exhausted, frustrated, and, in some cases, turning away from journalism altogether. They described work that brought harm to their physical and mental health, experiences of online abuse and harassment, precarious and unpaid labor, and the constant disruption of personal time. Yet journalists said they also felt pressure to "live online" to fulfill their professional obligations and advance their careers. The impact of reporting during the global pandemic only reinforced these pressures, as journalists reported feeling pressure to mediate the existing demands of their job with a growing responsibility to mitigate the effects of misinformation flows online.[6] In the absence of organizational support and policy from their employers about how to use social media, journalists told us they were negotiating increasingly complex forms of online connection and disconnection in their professional and personal lives.

The Paradox of Connection explores how journalists use strategies of connection and disconnection to mediate the impact of social media on their professional practice, professional identity, and professional purpose. We use the term "paradoxical" to highlight the often-nuanced nature of this online labor. For all the new and innovative forms of online connection that have changed professional practices, there have also been material impacts on journalists themselves. We argue that these impacts have led journalists to develop connection and disconnection practices that help foster safer and more productive forms of online connection rather than causing journalists to turn away from professional social media use altogether.

In this book, we address four aspects of journalists' connection and disconnection from social media: (1) how practices of connection and disconnection in social media environments are formed, negotiated, and maintained through journalistic practices, cultures, and institutions; (2) the ways journalists respond to organizational and institutional influences on social media labor; (3) the implications of social media connection and disconnection for journalists' relationships with audiences; and (4) how news organizations can adopt a systematic approach to disconnection as part of journalistic labor. Taking these key aspects as a starting point, we use journalists' experiences of connection and disconnection to critically analyze the rapidly transforming labor, practices, values, and competencies that constitute contemporary journalistic practice and professional identity.

Connection and Disconnection in Journalism Practice

Journalists, much like other workers in the knowledge economy, increasingly bring their profession into their personal spaces: on their laptops and phones when they travel, when they are at home, and when they are enjoying leisure time with friends and family. Checking a smartphone is often the very first and the very last thing journalists do each day.[7] The COVID-19 pandemic, which began in 2020, exacerbated this trend, especially with the rise of remote work and use of nonproprietary digital platforms like Zoom, the video communication tool, and Slack, the instant messaging program. The 2021 Reuters Institute for the Study of Journalism report showed that since the pandemic began, "many publishers are entering a new phase: the move from fully remote working to a hybrid set-up, with some people working from the newsroom and some working from home."[8] This practice has contributed to increasing journalists' individual professional autonomy, though this has come at a cost.[9] Some editors and managers have relinquished control to journalists, but this has often meant that the boundaries between work and personal time have become blurred. It has also meant that journalists are often dealing with the impacts of their work, including increasing online harassment, without organizational support.[10] Journalists have found ways to balance the impacts of the always-connected nature of online work, often through forms of disconnection.

Disconnection studies has emerged as a field that addresses both technical and cultural practices and politico-social frameworks for resistance to social media. Studies have included how individuals negotiate opting out and the avoidance or nonuse of social media, while others have explored the political dimensions of disconnection through political, technical, and consumer lenses.[11] Previous research implies the importance of disconnection in social media use by suggesting the ways that users create and break connections across multiple sites.[12] Other forms of temporary or permanent disconnection from social media platforms have included artistic or subversive acts of "digital suicide" and forms of reluctant digital participation or digital exclusion.[13]

Extending from these studies, we focus on disconnection in the context of professional journalism as the modes of disengagement individuals choose to avoid or mediate the connective affordances of social media.[14] Some disconnection tactics journalists often deploy to mediate connectivity include creating private spheres for interaction, not engaging with certain platforms or users, using technical boundaries like blocking or muting, and taking "micro breaks" from online connection.

It is nonetheless important to acknowledge the connective outcomes for many strategies of disconnection. We suggest that journalists, who often have no choice but to work on social media, use disconnection strategies and practices to negotiate, structure, and come to terms with living online. We use the term "negotiation" because it indicates that most online users continually respond to the technical, social, and cultural development of social media. Journalists, like other professional workers, experiment with different forms of connection and disconnection. The practices, values, and competencies that emerge are not—and have never been—fixed.[15] Instead, journalists constantly connect and disconnect with different relationships, practices, and institutional norms to adapt their work to changing media environments.

This book examines these practices as part of a continuum of connection and disconnection from social media that journalists continually negotiate to make online labor part of their everyday professional life. Journalists negotiate uses of social media according to professional needs, traditional boundaries of professional identity and ideology, challenges with structural inequalities, and the necessity to live and work productively within the perceived boundaries of digital labor.

Journalists engage with these forms of disconnection to better understand the intricacies of online interaction and to protect themselves from professional or personal harm. It is therefore important to acknowledge that disconnection and connection strategies do not align to binaries of use and nonuse of specific technologies or platforms. Disconnection might suggest solely negative consequences of journalists' online labor. However, continual negotiation of online connection also contributes to the potential for extended productive use of online and social media over time.[16] Similarly, journalists might limit social media connectivity to manage large audiences or maintain a particular online representation of the self, but these strategies also add value and individual meaning to online experiences.[17]

Journalism and Social Media: Framing the Transformation of Journalistic Labor

This book focuses on professional journalism, which we define as "the activity of gathering, assessing, creating, and presenting news and information. It is also the product of these activities."[18] We acknowledge, however, that both the activities and the products of journalism are complex, and they often vary in different global contexts. There is no doubt that levels of precarity have influenced contemporary journalism, where lack of control over resourcing and future work possibilities has led to shifts toward atypical labor formats, such as freelancing and digital-only news production.[19] Nonetheless, we argue that it is still paid—albeit notoriously underpaid and overworked—journalists who are largely responsible for the majority of mainstream news reportage, which is dependent on professional access to newsmakers and news events.

This book focuses on the everyday practice of professional journalism as well as the organizational, professional, and institutional structures that regulate and delimit the use of social media. By focusing on the labor of "everyday journalism," we recognize that the ways journalism is organizationally structured may be changing, but the institutional ideologies and values of journalism have endured. Journalists' values, behaviors, and strategies for creating and distributing news are still important in conveying relevant information to audiences. As many scholars contend, journalism is a field that is in perpetual transformation, but journalists' commitment to the "ideals of journalism" remains deeply entrenched in news work, and their boundaries are often protected from change.[20]

In this book, we refer to social media labor as work individuals do to source, research, produce, distribute, and analyze news content, as well as to promote journalism and journalists through different forms of online interactions with existing and potential audiences. This labor is affected by the "continuing market logic" within media industries, working conditions both enabled and limited by increasing "tech fetishization" and the increasing need for "affective labor" in online attention economies.[21]

Social media is defined as the numerous web-based applications or services that allow different forms of online communication and connection and enable users to create and share content as well as network. More specifically, social media allows individuals or groups to (1) construct and share representations of identities or events online through a public or semiprivate social networking profile; (2) create, view, share, or discuss content or social connections with other users; and (3) view, follow, and interact with the content and connections of other users.[22]

Much of the work that journalists do on social media is now part of the assumed labor of their role—though much of the associated relational labor of managing online interactions and engagement remains relatively unsupported by news organizations. This type of social media work is not exclusive to journalism and has become part of many professional routines. Social media work has developed a distinctive set of services, products, and forms of labor that revolve around the specific markets, audiences, and professions emerging from organizational use of social media.[23] While social media work might seem to be part of promotional or marketing strategies for organizations, it has developed to incorporate audience or community building, internal and external communications, media production, professional governance, and data analytics and insights.[24] At the same time, monetization of social media content through advertising, promotion, and influence has produced a burgeoning content creation industry where influencer marketing has created a new role for freelance and amateur media makers.[25]

The emergence of new media players such as web analytics companies and social media platform companies, as well as new technologies such as virtual reality tools, artificial intelligence, and machine learning, has challenged the role of professional journalism in informing the public. Conceptualization of journalism's professional boundaries has emphasized three things: the professional practices that produce journalism; the values and norms that identify the professional journalist; and the relationship between the journalist, their profession, and their audiences.[26] This discourse of professionalism presents a justification for journalists having a powerful role in the governance of society through a claim to represent or act on behalf of the "public."[27] It is only those who claim a professional and elite status through their expertise over these journalistic practices who can also claim social, cultural, or political authority to speak about—and for—the public interest.[28]

Scholars and practitioners have criticized discursive positioning of journalism for limiting opportunities to diversify approaches to journalism in newsrooms and for privileging the voices of the powerful in setting the news agenda. Pacinthe Mattar argues that objectivity is a privilege afforded to white journalists because "for many other journalists, there is no distance between what happened to George Floyd and what could have happened to them. Distance is a luxury."[29] The objectivity principle has also contributed to journalists' and organizations' resistance to change around diversifying the workforce. More traditional newsrooms have been hesitant to adopt innovative practices because of their fear of increased cost or loss of editorial control or their hesitancy to challenge traditionally held news values.[30]

Much of the scholarship on journalistic professionalism online has also suggested that journalists often attempt to "normalize" professional occupational ideologies, even within new media practices.[31] Jane Singer suggests that this normalization process either applies journalists' existing patterns and routines to new media formats or creates new professional norms that account for the new digital affordances of these platforms.[32] Innovation in using social media in journalism has focused on the individual labor of journalists using social media profiles to source, produce, and promote news stories. It has also emphasized organizational use of social media, especially employment of community managers and analytics tools.[33]

Other studies have investigated the potential of social media to contribute to new forms of journalism such as social, citizen, and activist reporting for specific communities.[34] Journalistic uses of social media have also influenced news production values, including increasing prioritization of the audience and interactivity of news content; participation of audiences in news; transparency in news production processes; immediate, twenty-four-hour dissemination of news on social media; and reliance on a specific platform such as the microblogging platform Twitter or the mobile chat application WhatsApp.[35]

While much of the early research about social media assumed that the normalization of journalistic practices on social media would have a positive effect on both journalists and their audiences, complicating factors have emerged.[36] A number of productive tensions have led to changes in journalistic work and more diversity in practices that make up journalistic culture.[37] New ways of sharing and consuming media mean that journalistic boundaries around who makes the news are becoming much more porous. They have also allowed for new, misrepresented, or previously ignored voices in the news to create new forms of news and information sharing. For example, *Indigenous X*, a news organization owned and operated by Indigenous Australians, has gained mainstream popularity because of its focus on upholding Indigenous voices and knowledge in news production.[38] This has led Oscar Westlund to argue that traditional forms of professional identity construction might not be as relevant in the online and mobile media age due to the audience-centric and participation-centric focus of news media making and consumption.[39]

Many of these changes have been widely explored in the media and in academic research, but this discussion has not always considered the impacts of this transition on journalists attempting to balance the organizational pressures of being online with their own professional norms and expectations.[40] Further research has shown the unintended impacts of social media labor on journalists, including increased workload, online harassment, and feelings of burnout.[41] Emerging global research has also explored mental health and well-being in journalism, especially the vast literature on harassment. The impacts of these issues have also led to forms of disconnection from social media, which have so far not been explored.

At the 2018 International Communication Association (ICA) conference in Washington, DC, we decided to bring our separate areas of expertise together to think more about how journalists could work online safely, supported by media organizations and the industry more broadly. We wanted to understand the everyday experiences of journalists impacted by these changes and, by doing so, to advocate for organizational and institutional change. We argue that the foundation for change in the media industry is an institutional, organizational, and policy framework that centers and shares empathetic approaches to digital work. This framework would support not only journalists but also all workers who suddenly find themselves living online.

The Paradox of Connection: An Overview

The Paradox of Connection builds on years of qualitative interviews, surveys, and observational studies based on our research about the transformation of journalism practice and professional identity over time. We identify as journalism studies scholars conducting interdisciplinary, empirical research conceptually framed by media sociology, sociology of work and organizations, media management, and media studies literature to shed light on the identities, practices, and norms that make up contemporary journalism. Our previous research has noted transformational changes in journalism organizational cultures, policies, and social media work practices that have had material impacts on both newsrooms and journalists themselves.

We recorded the experiences of journalists using mixed methods, including interviews and observation, drawing on more than one hundred semi-structured interviews with journalists from 2016 to 2021.[42] The purpose of the interviews was to consider the often-complex relationship between identity representation, social media cultures, and professional practices. We recruited journalist participants from across Australia, the United States, and elsewhere who represented diversity in terms of ethnicity, gender identification, media role, and professional seniority. To ensure that journalist participants were active users, we verified that they had at least a thousand followers on social media and posted at least once every two days. We conducted interviews using a semi-structured approach, and we gave participants a random identifier in the transcription. We analyzed the deidentified interview responses using a grounded approach, with themes hand-coded as they emerged. This process was purposely ongoing and iterative to allow for dynamic comparison, and we used knowledge organization frameworks to ensure consistency and specificity of analysis.

To extend the reflections provided in interviews with journalists, we also conducted policy analysis, large-scale surveys, and online content analysis. As Martin Hand suggests, social media content is not simply representation but also a means of circulation, a mode of social participation, and a site for professional and personal practices.[43] Thus, content posted on social media cannot be treated as direct evidence; instead, it must be viewed as a mediated, partial account requiring contextual reflection. We used an inductive approach to analyze these data, defining key concepts from the experiences described by journalists and combining these concepts with analysis of newsroom policy and content. Policy and observational analysis also allowed conceptualization to attend closely to professional contexts while allowing flexibility to include additional new observation. Overall, the data speak to the lived experience of journalists seeking to nuance their connective practices, the unique issues they face in connecting journalism to audiences in social media spaces, and how disconnection strategies are used to mediate these issues.[44] We have conceptualized this analysis within three different elements of connection and disconnection in this book.

Part I defines the paradoxical conceptualization of social media connection and disconnection in journalism. Chapters 1 and 2 look at modes of connection in journalism and its interrelation with strategies of disconnection.

Chapter 1, "Journalism and the Paradox of Connection," focuses on defining forms of connection—commercial, professional, and civic—that have emerged from journalists' work on social media. Increasing professionalization of social media spaces has encouraged journalists and news organizations to present an always-on presence alongside the representation of an "authentic" online persona and more intimate engagement with audiences. Journalists, like other media workers, have now constructed and maintained professional online personas that brand their news reportage and themselves by including aspects of their personal lives such as their individual character, details of their lives, or opinions and interests.[45] Journalists also have incorporated more civic and reciprocal forms of connection with audiences, mediating their online personas with more traditional professional purpose. This chapter shows how individual mediation of the potential influence of social media and its impact on journalists has led to different professional strategies for connection online.

Chapter 2, "Burning Out, Turning Off, and Disconnecting," discusses the disconnection strategies journalists use to navigate use of social media in media work. Extending our arguments from chapter 1, we argue in chapter 2 that new forms of social media work designed to maintain connection have also led to frustration among journalists about (1) the perception of increased affective labor; (2) dissatisfaction with communication environments on particular social media platforms; and (3) increased anxiety about the possible impact of social media use on both their professional reputations and their personal well-being. Using interviews with professional journalists, chapter 2 illustrates that experiences of social media fatigue have resulted in a careful renegotiation of professional and personal boundaries around journalists' social media use influenced by the technological, social, and cultural affordances of specific media platforms, organizational and institutional constraints, and the online literacies and behaviors of journalists themselves.

In part II we move from the conceptualization of connection and disconnection to empirical analyses of how these strategies manifest across journalists' relationships with organizations, audiences, and institutional epistemologies.

Chapter 3, "Maintaining Professional Connections through Branding," focuses on the online branding strategies journalists use to maintain a professional and organizational identity in online and social media spaces. As journalists integrate social media into their professional work, they wrestle with how best to represent themselves, their organizations, and their profession. This chapter explores the use of branding practices to connect with current and potential news audiences on social media, that is, the levels at which such branding occurs, whether to promote oneself (individual), one's news organization (organizational), or the journalism profession more broadly (institutional).[46]

Chapter 4, "Dis/connecting from Policy and Practice," turns to a more practice-based understanding of newsroom structure and policy. As new technologically oriented work practices and actors emerge, journalists have increasingly been tasked with learning new practices, organizational procedures, and professional behaviors. Journalists have also had to work with new organizational policies, new newsroom actors, and new online audiences. But these policies do not always adequately address these tensions and in many cases can't accomplish what they set out to do. This chapter conceptualizes the ways newsroom social media policies shape connection and disconnection strategies among journalists while governing, or attempting to govern, their online and social media practices.

In part III we focus on the types of connections and disconnections that frame journalists' work practices in social media environments.

Chapter 5, "Connecting with Journalism in an Era of Misinformation," explores some of the consequences of more intimate and engaged strategies of connection with news audiences. This chapter focuses on the more disruptive and confrontational forms of engagement that come with professional use of social media for journalism. It explores how misinformation and disinformation on social media point to some of the larger issues around changing modes of connection between journalists and audiences and of disconnection from broader social norms around journalism's professional ideologies. Using case studies related to reportage on the COVID-19 pandemic, this chapter unpacks some of the strategies journalists have used to engage with dynamic online publics and to negotiate new forms of online interaction in order to safely and productively participate within online cultures that prioritize authenticity and sometimes deliberately disruptive content.

Building on the previous chapters, chapter 6, "Harassment and Disconnection in Journalism's Digital Labor," shows how traditional norms of public dialogue—framed by professional ideologies and governmental and legal norms—have become sites of contestation in online spaces as audiences resist or re-create the power structures that frame public dialogue, sometimes in deliberately defamatory ways, such as trolling and flaming. Journalists themselves are often engaging with or being targeted by the deliberately defamatory commentary and discussion that are seemingly part of online news flows and often posted without any legal repercussions. With a focus on harassment, this chapter illustrates the disconnection practices that have allowed individual journalists to cope with online harassment while making recommendations for media organizations to establish a more systemic approach to deal with online abuse of journalists.

The conclusion conceptualizes frameworks of online connection and disconnection within broader understandings of media work and the implications for the platforms, audiences, media organizations, and creative industries engaged with online and social media environments. Questions of connection and disconnection are clearly broader than journalism: new forms of journalistic work engendered by social media technologies, techniques, and cultures should be contextualized by conceptions of new forms of online labor overall. The dynamism of social media spaces reconfigures the context for private and public interactions; thus, the spaces for work, pleasure, and engagement are becoming increasingly complex.[47] Finally, we outline some of the impacts of these new frameworks for media work on the constitution of journalism and ways forward to increase journalism's online accuracy, safety, and relevance in the future.

Defining Connection and Disconnection in Journalism

CHAPTER 1

Journalism and the Paradox of Connection

As the COVID-19 virus accelerated into what became an unstoppable spread across the globe, the public thirst for news and information also grew exponentially. Journalists suddenly found themselves thrown into round-the-clock crisis reporting, working within government health orders that restricted movement and contextualizing complex epidemiological information for public understanding. Journalists expected that their reportage would foster deep connections with audiences unified by the experience of an unprecedented health crisis. What they were less prepared for was finding themselves targeted by public anger and mistrust about governmental responses to the pandemic. One Australian journalist said that the onslaught of online information, misinformation, and political machinations—dubbed an "infodemic"—resulted in public anger being directed at journalists as the traditional messengers and translators of public events: "There was so much anger online and aimed at the daily press conferences. People began to tune out because of the politics. People don't want to be told how to feel about the facts because they were already feeling a million emotions."[1]

To counter this public angst, many journalists reported working the longest and most arduous hours of their careers. British journalists reported work overload, anxiety, and frustration about that workload and a growing negative public perception of journalists.[2] Similarly, Belgian journalists reported feelings of frustration at worsening work conditions.[3] Ghanaian journalists reported high anxiety about contracting the virus or infecting their families in the course of their work and the difficulty of prioritizing objective and impartial reporting during a period of public fear.[4] The one thing that connected these journalists was that they said they balanced these negative impacts with feelings of professional purpose stemming from the public importance of their work.

At a time when journalism's public role should have been undeniable, these journalists' experiences tell us much about the paradoxical nature of online connection. There is no doubt that connection has become a catch-all term for the idealization of social media use. Sharing ideas with others while being free from the limits of geography, time, or social status has long been the aspirational vision for the internet. For journalists, making online connections with sources, audiences, and other professional newsmakers also fulfills one of the professional purposes of journalism: to ensure social impact through public engagement with their work.

The ongoing COVID-19 pandemic has shown how powerful the lure of online connection is to journalists' professional purpose. The rise of professional and personal social media use across the globe has meant that making these connections, at least initially, is easier. Yet journalists continually report that fostering these online connections during the pandemic has had negative impacts on their physical and mental health, along with their sense of professional satisfaction.[5] An International Federation of Journalists survey showed that 70 percent of respondents indicated that the most difficult aspect of their work during the pandemic was its psychological and emotional toll.[6] Along with the material impacts of increased labor during the pandemic, journalists reported that online environments fostered misinformation, disinformation, and continued harassment of journalists. One study of UK journalists showed that digital environments created a sense of relentless emotional labor to deal with the public thirst for information and the subsequent public negativity around reportage of the crisis.[7]

As outlined in this book's introduction, increasing professionalization of social media spaces has encouraged journalists and news organizations to move much of the labor of connecting with audiences to online spaces. News consumption has increasingly moved to online and social media spaces; thus, news organizations and journalists have responded by presenting an always-online presence, which has had an impact on the news media ecosystem worldwide. The UK-based news organization *The Guardian* omitted print publication entirely when it introduced its news product to the United States in 2011 and Australia in 2013, opting to offer live coverage of politics and daily events on the blog-style front page of its website.[8] In the past decade, a plethora of mobile-only news apps, including aggregators such as *AppleNews* and *Flipboard*, have emerged and become important sites of news consumption.

Creating an always-on presence online requires a different conceptualization of journalistic labor by news organizations. This new form of labor balances traditional journalistic values with continual online availability for connection to audiences and responsiveness to metrics-driven analysis of journalists' work. Sustaining this online connection with audiences over time requires something even more: it requires journalists to give something of themselves. As Nancy Baym suggests, online connection allows more personalized forms of communication and identity expression to reach much larger groups. Baym argues that these more intimate forms of communication have increasingly become the predominant form of connection for social media.[9] As journalists have increasingly adopted these more personal forms of communication, fostering connection within social media spaces has complicated the purpose, function, and practice of journalism.

New forms of online labor have created more competing interests from other online actors, more organizational and professional demands for intimate and authentic connection, and more reputational and safety impacts from increased online commentary and engagement.

This chapter explores what these different forms of connection mean for journalists. We conceptualize the forms of connection—commercial, professional, and civic—that have emerged from journalists' work on social media and the context through which they might arise. Using interviews conducted with journalists about their posting practices and additional data from journalists globally, this chapter shows how journalists develop professional strategies to foster connection on social media. We also show how new forms of professional labor associated with fostering online connection, such as building online personas, engaging with online communities, and commercializing content, have also led to increasing use of strategies of disconnection. This chapter provides the conceptual framework for the rest of the book, which focuses on how journalists negotiate the impact of connection by using strategic forms of disconnection in different cultural, organizational, political, and personal contexts.

Defining Social Media Connection

We define online connection in terms of both the technical affordance of being connected through the internet to a network infrastructure and the activities of connection afforded by social and cultural affordance, which both allow a communicative interaction to create and share information within online communities and networks. We use the term "social media connection" in this book to refer to different activities that encourage, form, and maintain a communicative relationship between individuals or groups of social media users. Forms of online "engagement" and "interaction" include the activities of attracting and maintaining connection on social media.

These terms reflect patterns of collaboration and exchange rather than the patterns of production and consumption often associated with mass media. The motivation, intent, and desired outcome of these forms of connection are contextual and often dynamic according to individual, organizational, and technical influences. Both the technical affordances and user mediation of these affordances affect the types of connection that are possible on specific platforms. As cultures of use develop and are popularized on platforms, individuals and groups will use and negotiate the kinds of connections that are encouraged and then integrate them into their personal and professional lives. In other words, negotiation of technological affordances and the cultures that emerge from platforms contributes to shaping the forms of connection that emerge on social media.

Building forms of community through social media connection beyond the limitations of geography, time, or socioeconomic status has been at the forefront of platform innovation. While individuals have long used media such as public letters and radio broadcasts to express themselves and discuss issues, social media technologies allow easy and inexpensive creation and instantaneous sharing on a global scale.[10] The opportunities for individuals to access tools to create and share content and the increasingly everyday nature of sharing information about personal lives have undoubtedly changed the nature of our relation to public life.[11] The selfie, an image taken by a user of themselves specifically to post on social media and that can be traced to the Victorian camera, is an example of the merging of mass public communication and personal individual expression that has influenced new communicative cultures on social media platforms.[12] Sharing personal images and information has become an everyday but nonetheless central aspect of social media culture. Forms of intimacy and sharing appear to be part of a performative culture of self-expression, which Charles Fairchild suggests has resulted in an attention economy where audience attention is assigned value on the platform.[13] Concern with and promotion of individual visibility is a kind of affective, entrepreneurial labor that can be leveraged into social and economic capital.[14]

While the introduction of new affordances on social media platforms has fostered their own vernacular cultures of use, the context has often been the same: to connect users into communities based on individual need or interest. For example, Instagram's technical capabilities prioritizing aesthetic imagery has helped foster ingroup knowledge around its aesthetic and discursive norms.

These cultural norms have recognizable vernaculars, such that the correct use of filters, hashtags, and tagging practices builds forms of connection around sharing these modes of visual expression.[15] Over time, these modes of connection have been articulated through performances of authentic self-presentation, which allow intimate narratives of self to become public.[16]

For some users, the popularity of self-expression is valuable as a form of social status that can be commodified. Influencer commerce and culture has resulted in new online practices, particularly among young women.[17] In particular, influencers perform visibility labor, aiming to demonstrate self-conspicuousness or popular attention, generally for the purpose of commodification.[18] These forms of labor are defined as microcelebrity, a particular mindset on social media where self-presentation practices are created to appear authentic and intimate, though they are more likely to be strategic and curated to engage potential followers and improve online popularity.[19] Microcelebrity refers not only to popular social media users but also to the capacity for attention garnered by individual social media users who brand and/or commodify their unique online personas. Practices of microcelebrity have been somewhat maligned; while they make it possible for regular users to attract large audiences based on their personal self-expression, many popular users tend to portray conventional tropes of cool, including glamour, conventional beauty standards, and luxury aspiration (see chapter 5).

While not everyone on social media aspires to be an influencer, forms of commodified identity representation and sharing behavior have been adopted by regular users, including the use of vernacular such as tags, reposts, popular hashtags such as #instagood, and platform-specific in-jokes such as the use of the peach emoji to represent a person's backside. This usage is underlined by the technical architecture and affordances of social media platforms, which encourage constant sharing to foster connection that is attached to highly visible metrics of success, such as the number of followers or likes attached to content.[20] The professionalization of social media connection has meant that many of these social norms have been co-opted into professional, promotional, or commercial imperatives.

Journalists, like many other media workers, have leveraged modes of social media connection to align with their own professional practices. This has often meant moving away from traditional journalistic methods of representation and adapting communication skills to correspond with social and behavioral norms that gain attention within specific social media cultures. Journalists have thus modified traditional reporting practices to include particular modes of self-expression and self-presentation that garner attention within a culture of practices that values both authenticity and attention-getting strategies.[21]

In this book, we conceptualize connection in the context of journalists' different professional practices on social media. This is because we want to highlight the fact that the formation and maintenance of different forms of connection are a new part of a journalist's work practices and professional labor. There are several reasons for this. First, the transition of professional journalistic practice to social media environments has undoubtedly been a challenge for journalists. Previous research has shown that journalists have struggled with both the adoption of new online platforms for communication and the pressure to engage with more dynamic online publics. Second, this new form of labor has been normalized within unrealistic workflows in organizational contexts. While much research has situated social media as enabling new forms of journalistic practice that are increasingly collaborative and that prioritize authentic and transparent processes of presenting the news, other research has found that these changes require ongoing conformity to particular technical skills and appropriate online behaviors.[22] Jodi Dean has indicated how communicative capitalism repurposes important democratic ideals to support commercialization of ideals of participation and transparency.[23] In the context of journalism, social media policies, metrics, and labor expectations converge to impact how journalists work. With increasing use of social media, journalists have had to negotiate what Melissa Gregg terms the "presence bleed" of communication technologies into otherwise private spaces and the "function creep" of online connections once meant to sustain friendships being used to engage audiences for professional outcomes.[24] Social media connection has often been conceptualized through these new forms of creative, informational, and affective social media work. In this context, journalistic work has expanded to include growing online followings for professional purposes. This has included additional labor to post, comment, and engage with users; promote news content and organizations; and brand professional identities. We want to highlight that these practices change and develop according to many different influences, including a specific platform's technological and cultural affordances, as well as the types of connection practices that are most relevant to a journalist's professional and organizational needs.

Conceptualizing Social Media Connection in Journalism

This book conceptualizes two different kinds of social connection enacted by journalists with different professional outcomes. These behaviors may be grouped as follows: first, professional branding and promotional work, whether focused on an individual online persona or news organizations or for the purposes of commercialization of news products; and second, establishing civic reciprocity within online communities of interest. We acknowledge that these are not discrete categories; indeed, the interconnection between them is important, as it shows that the negotiation of social media technologies and cultures has often been an individual endeavor by journalists influenced by different organizational and institutional contexts.

An important difference between these categories is the implied difference in conceptualization of the audience by the journalist. In our research we saw a marked difference in each of these forms of connection according to whether journalists conceptualized audiences as news consumers, as fans or followers, or as members of a community to which the journalist belongs. When journalists imagined an audience to be based on news consumption, their corresponding social media behavior was more promotional and transactional. When journalists imagined followers of their individual profile, their interactions are focused on practices suited to an attention economy. Finally, when journalists imagined an audience to be composed of fellow community members, their practices of connection were more reciprocal or collaborative.

In our interviews with journalists and our observations during our own respective research about their posting practices on social media, we saw these different forms of connection emerge through the negotiation of complex and interconnected influences on journalists. An understanding of personal identity, a reliance on the traditional ideology of professional practice, and editorial and institutional pressures all affect the ways journalists use social media, the way they engage with their audiences, and, by extension, the way audiences engage with them.

The first kind of connection occurs when journalists brand their professional identity and encourage a user connection that links back to organizational outcomes. This type of connection refers to journalists' increasing acknowledgment of the metrics-based focus on audience engagement in contemporary newsrooms. Similarly, the algorithmic sorting of content on social media platforms can mean either a hit or complete ignorance of a news story. Much of the contemporary distribution and consumption of news is now happening regardless of the influence of news organizations; therefore, the effects of individual journalists' promotion of clicks, likes, and eyeballs have become much more important parts of practice. News organizations are employing social media trainers to personalize journalists' dissemination of news, and countless online resources assist journalists wanting to establish an online presence and improve their market value.

An individual journalist's connection with audiences can influence clickthrough rates to the journalism produced and posted on major news organizations' websites. It can also assist journalists to promote their own work within an industry environment marked by employment precarity. Therefore, journalists, like other media industry workers, have constructed and maintained professional online personas that brand their news reportage and themselves by including aspects of their personal lives, opinions, and interests.[25] The forms of connection established by these journalists on social media thus center around a professional persona or brand that promotes an individual journalist's reportage or their media organization.

Reflecting a broader global trend, reporters revealed that they develop a specific communication tone and content style for social media because they realized that doing so appealed more to the new audience segments they were trying to attract. This perception of audiences focuses on their value as news consumers in terms of both gaining eyeballs toward a news organization's content and improving distribution of a journalist's reportage through online sharing. One rural reporter said: "I tried straight-up journalism. I started that way, and you don't get much reaction. I've realized that it needs to be a slightly different voice and that you can be playful and let your personality come out. . . . I'm just trying to imagine the people who are following me, that if I can present a bit of our show, my colleagues, and . . . a bit about the programs in general to new audiences."[26] As shown in chapters 3 and 5, this change of tone to incorporate professional identity branding has become a typical journalistic use of social media that identifies specific branding practices, such as the use of humor, audience engagement, and personal information.[27] Some journalists post behind-the-scenes images or humorous banter with news crews and other journalists. These strategies show a lighter side of reporting and a journalist's personality—and they allow a journalist to switch to more considered discussion (and promotion) of reportage when required.[28]

Related to professional and organizational branding practices is connection based on establishing an individually commercialized persona on social media. A journalist may leverage influencer culture to build an individually recognizable brand persona that is distinguishable from a news organization. This provides other content opportunities, such as commercialized or individual production ventures. Journalists will also borrow far more heavily from social media cultures of connection to brand themselves and news products they wish to further commercialize. This is seen increasingly with entrepreneurial journalistic ventures such as freelance journalism, journalists working with subscription-based business models, or journalists increasingly blurring the line between journalism and promotion.

A small number of journalists we spoke to tagged brand names and used tags like #sponpost to show that they had pursued an additional commercial benefit from promoting certain events or products. Similarly, a small group of journalists interviewed said that they had Instagram-led side projects, including creating paid content. Other journalists appeared to act as brand ambassadors or to run side businesses based on paid expertise or advice. For example, a travel journalist had set up a side business led by Instagram and other social media content that provided advice and expertise about working in the travel industry, selling the opportunity for people to travel for free by making rich media content. Another journalist suggested that the intent of this individual commercialization of social media content, which stemmed from their previous role at a digital-first organization, is to create branded content, pitching news story ideas that the sales team could then sell to advertisers as social campaigns, articles, and podcasts. While each of the journalists interviewed suggested that the practices are journalistic, none of these fit easily into traditional categorization of journalistic professional norms or behaviors.

Many of the practices used by journalists borrowed more heavily from the aspirational glamour popularized by social media influencers who post images within particular aesthetic framing and use in-group knowledge to connect with other like-minded users about their fashion and lifestyle reportage: "If I posted a red-carpet photo on Instagram, I get a heap of likes, and people will say, 'I love the dress.'... That does let your audience get a little bit closer to you, and then they may in turn engage more with your content."[29] While this might seem contrived, a fashion journalist suggests that the changes in content and tone are more about relating to the specific cultural mores of a particular platform. Conceiving of online audiences as followers who are interested in individual journalists allows connections that adhere more to the social and cultural affordances of the specific platform itself. This helps to maintain relevance and influence in spaces where journalists are not necessarily the go-to authorities on news and information.[30] In this context, fostering connections with users around areas of interest is a much more important aspect of journalistic labor. Access to these communities of interest may obscure the promotional intent of these forms of connection, though that promotional intent is generally accepted by followers if they enjoy the content. These seemingly backstage aspects of journalists' personal lives attempt to foster an intimate connection that can be leveraged toward promotion of other products. To this end, a political journalist said they posted images of themselves in glamorous outfits because it garnered attention around their life as a journalist, which was useful in promoting their recently published biography.

The profound mediatization of everyday life has resulted in intimate relationships with media technologies, prioritizing the role of relationships between people and online content.[31] This means that journalists who generally have no choice but to promote themselves online may gain more professional satisfaction through a sense of genuine and reciprocal audience connection.[32] The relationships that content creators form through the emotional and relational labor of caring can be rewarding and pleasurable, often because it connects users through appreciation of professional work and genuine connection through shared interests. This does not negate that this authenticity is a saleable branding of identity.[33] However, for those who are tied to online labor or provision of online content, forms of care for audiences can humanize the labor associated with journalistic role performance online.[34]

A television broadcaster reported that they spent over an hour per day using different social media platforms to post videos and images and to comment on and like their followers' posts. There was no professional requirement for the effort they were making to connect with otherwise random followers; however, the broadcaster said that these small acts of connection were a new way to communicate: "We've never had this opportunity to speak directly with our audiences and find out what they think—it's really exciting."[35] The broadcast journalist here is referring to the pleasure received through social media connection for connection's sake, that is, the more traditional journalistic sense of professional purpose fostered through social media connection.

While branding and commercialization techniques are a common use of social media, some journalists have found that this can foster a kind of one-way or perhaps extractive form of connection. This has resulted in some news organizations taking a more editorial approach to social media management within the newsroom, using community managers to support the sourcing and dissemination of news, and providing industry-centered training around journalistic use of social media. Journalists have also incorporated more civic and reciprocal forms of connection with audiences, maintaining a professional purpose linked to expression of a traditional journalistic ideology and identity.

Prioritizing forms of connection has not simply emerged with increasing use of online tools but has long been part of journalistic labor. Journalists often speak of their "connection" to an issue as an important part of their beat or as something they have continually researched and reported on. Journalists similarly talk about fostering a deep connection to a community through audiences impacted directly by reportage. In this context, audiences are perceived more as a "community" that needs to be served by access to good information and discussion about news of interest. This might initially seem to foster a kind of one-way connection, where the journalist uses the online space to further their own reportage. For example, a finance journalist said that if they weren't a journalist, they wouldn't connect to audiences on social media at all. They have used social media as a useful journalism tool for understanding the public interest in an issue or event: "I think that it's a good way to get a barometer of what's happening, what people are talking about, what conversations are kind of bubbling away. You get a kind of, like, what's happening today in terms of culture and news and generally what's interesting, the public's view today."[36] This type of social media use may seem limited in engagement potential, but it is nonetheless useful to journalists who said they monitored discussions, trending topics, and hashtags to get a better sense of what audiences might be interested in.

Other journalists connect more to communities of interest to be more collaborative about what they report. Reciprocity in online environments refers to online community understandings, such as common ties for shared beliefs, values, and cultural habits.[37] Online environments are increasingly dominated by practices of mutual sharing and distribution of information with significant implications for journalism practice, such as reciprocal journalism, which positions journalists as "community-builders who might catalyze reciprocal exchange—directly with audiences/users, indirectly among community members, and repeatedly over time, altogether encouraging the kind of social norms associated with reciprocity."[38] In this regard, audiences are perceived as collaborative community members who share relatively similar interests with journalists in the civic purpose of accessing quality news and information.

Connection practices that are reciprocal are a mutually beneficial form of support and exchange central to both journalists and the wider social frameworks of platforms. A sense of reciprocity in sharing can also provide a more professionally satisfying sense of engagement with communities. Collectively, these practices help to align journalists' public service ideals with the social media labor integral to maintaining relevance within ever-changing and media-saturated environments. Investigative journalists in Beijing, for example, often cocreate ongoing news investigations with audiences through the phenomenon of plot twist reporting, which provides incremental reporting that contradicts facts provided by government sources. This helps audiences interpret different versions of narrated truth and drives journalistic investigation in a difficult governmental context.[39] Due to the difficulty of finding alternate media voices in China, an Australian political reporter suggested that while they kept their persona on social media "strictly professional," their focus on reportage on politics in China draws a small but dedicated group of social media followers: "They followed me for a reason, not because they're my friend. They followed me because they're interested in my stories, or they're interested in the topics that I'm writing about. So it's sort of what I'm trying to keep to, whether it's business or China, I think they want to hear insights into more of that stuff. For example, if I'm at a sort of really important event like the opening of China's Congress, a really spectacular and historic event, I would post a couple of pictures from there."[40]

Some journalists we spoke to also fostered a collaborative approach to social media connection through sharing of resources. This may occur when journalists use their links to other users as a tool for their own journalism and maintain these connections through sharing information and discussion as a public contribution to these online communities. Other journalists we talked to used these forms of connection to enact a more traditional sense of professional purpose in social media environments. A data journalist said they shared some of the raw numbers behind some of their investigations with a small community of interested followers on Twitter: "I think because it is [data journalism it is] something which has a very sort of niche interest in our community."[41] This sharing sometimes resulted in larger discussions of the journalist's investigations and, occasionally, source material for follow-up stories. This reciprocity of data sharing, discussion, and analysis was a useful way for the journalist to promote their reportage and contribute to an interested online community.

The negotiation of journalistic practice to incorporate these new forms of interaction with audiences, often driven by market forces, organizational needs, and institutional ideals within ever-changing platform cultures and vernaculars, provides both opportunities and challenges to journalistic practice.[42] Reportage during the COVID-19 pandemic highlighted how connection with online publics once again fostered new journalistic uses of social media and new impacts across individual, organizational, and institutional influences. For instance, Vietnamese journalists partnered with science researchers and key government health agencies to quickly spread health information on social media, improving overall preparedness for the pandemic in Vietnam.[43] Other journalists reported using personal social media accounts to field public questions about the pandemic or fact-check links sent to their mobile phones.[44] These new uses of social media during the pandemic resulted in journalists viewing their work as "relentless and exhausting, where professional and personal boundaries no longer existed and where feelings of personal vulnerability were intensified."[45] Similarly, Eyewitness Media Hub has referred to newsrooms as a new "digital frontline" where journalists work in similar ways to crisis or war reporters and suffer impacts on their own physical and mental health as a result.[46] Further issues of increased labor, identification and verification of misinformation and so-called fake news, increased organizational jurisdiction over content on social media accounts, and intrusion into personal life and time have emerged in this evolving space. Increasingly, journalists have turned to forms of disconnection from social media platforms and audiences to mediate some of these new impacts on their professional and personal lives.

Defining Disconnection from Social Media

Disconnection from forms of social media connection is positioned as a mediating influence on the connective power of social media. In other words, finding ways to disconnect from social media platforms and engagements within those platforms can improve individual social media connectivity. Muting comments to avoid unwanted online interactions, blocking some users for brief periods of time as relief from their messaging without fully cutting off a relationship, silencing social media notifications before family meals, and taking more extended breaks from the overload of social media—these can all be part of disconnection.

Scholars tend to discuss the relationship between forms of social media connection and disconnection in terms of the binary opposites of the positive and negative impacts of social media. This is generally because initial engagement, participation, and connection narratives were central to the positioning of online and digital media early on as an improvement of our social lives.[47] Innovation in the use of social media is often premised on improving participation and engagement online. Facebook's relaunch as Meta in 2021, for example, saw the global organization's mission change, somewhat controversially, to giving "people the power to build community and bring the world closer together."[48]

There is no doubt that the initial celebration of social media as a utopian public square designed to improve sharing of ideas, cultures, and social life has been dampened by the actual experience of social media connection. Vulnerable and minority groups report the rise of harassment and discrimination from online trolls, and children report suffering from bullying and the impact of poor online body image representation. Unmitigated political disinformation and misinformation campaigns have swayed the course of elections, and even the platform companies themselves have been embroiled in countless data protection and privacy scandals. The ensuing techlash against these impacts has galvanized criticism of social media and in one popularized instance positioned it as a "social dilemma."[49] The 2020 Netflix docufiction *The Social Dilemma*, directed by Jeff Orlowski, focuses on how social media companies algorithmically manipulate users in ways that encourage addiction to these companies' platforms, allowing them to harvest users' personal data. The platforms have so far gone largely unregulated and have responded slowly or inadequately to calls for reform, including a global fact-checking movement. In place of celebration, many people's response to social media has been to digitally detox, meaning to turn away from or turn off social media connections altogether.

The development of disconnection studies has attempted to understand many of the complex facets of technology nonuse or media refusal.[50] Initially, disconnection was used to refer to an involuntary lack of access to digital technologies due to geographic, political, or socioeconomic issues.[51] Implicit in these early studies was that online connection was universally desired and that simply being online would achieve more inclusive social outcomes.[52] Further research has explored more socially and politically motivated nonparticipation in online environments, such as digital suicide, which refers to purposeful deletion of all online user information.[53] Other more ambiguous types of disconnection, such as passive participation, where users view but do not engage with online content, have shown that nonparticipation can be an active and complex practice.[54]

These differing accounts of disconnection have led others to suggest that describing binaries of use and nonuse of online technologies does not capture the nuance of users' motivations and social context in negotiating different forms of connection to online media.[55] Popular discussion of digital detox has been criticized for prioritizing individual wellness over understanding of complex social contexts for online participation.[56] Trine Syversten and Gunn Enli's analysis of self-help literature and corporate websites found that better personal and professional time management was prioritized as the best way to counter the negative impacts of online interactions.[57] Detoxing is thus positioned as an act of self-regulation where individual workers take personal responsibility for negotiating use of social media tools, even in professional environments where nonuse of social media would not be possible.[58]

Accounts of digital reluctance do not always consider just how ubiquitous, interconnected, and enmeshed our digital lives are, especially on social media. For professional media content producers like journalists, long periods of disconnection from social media would be almost impossible. As Mark Deuze suggests, media use is so ingrained in our lives that it has become invisible: "People do not recognize their media habits because they are a constitutive part of them."[59] So deeply bound is social media use in the everyday professional lives of journalists that negotiation of individual online practices is often seen as the only option. More recent work in disconnection studies has thus illustrated more of the context and motivation for nonparticipation in online spaces. This has included work on platform-specific disconnection, disconnection in professional contexts, and the positive and negative impacts of disconnection strategies.[60]

Our book extends Ben Light's conceptualization of disconnection as a series of possible decisions that may be (1) technological, that is, turning to or from a platform, its features, or its connections between sites; (2) algorithmic, that is, making decisions or influencing prioritization of people or content on platforms; (3) access-driven, that is, choices about what resource and access investments to make in online connection; (4) temporal, that is, choices about time spent on connection and disconnection on particular platforms; and (5) social and cultural.[61]

We conceptualize these decisions as occurring along a continuum, developing as their interconnection with other influences changes in particular spaces and times. Underlying these practices, there are also forms of connection and disconnection that are imbued with power—the ways we negotiate, choose, or are compelled to make forms of connection and disconnection. These might be influenced by things as diverse as personal ethics, organizational policy to platform sign-up requirements, and user posting rules, but they are nonetheless at the heart of these practices.[62]

Therefore, we refer to disconnection as distinct from terms like "turning off" social media connection and "digital detox." While these terms often relate to individual practices, disconnection and, by extension, disconnection studies as a growing discipline refer to the technical, social, and structural contexts and nuanced motivations for use and nonuse of social media. As Tero Karppi and colleagues suggest, individual practices of disconnection do not get to the context through which disconnection must exist.[63] This context includes the value placed on users' individual attention, the commodification of social bonds encouraged by both platform companies and media employers, and the centrality of forms of online connection to our professional and personal lives.

In this context, it can be difficult for individual media workers like journalists to forward acts of resistance against the imposition of social media logics in their professional lives. We therefore acknowledge that disconnection occurs in the context of journalism as "living with" social media rather than resisting or disrupting its connective bonds.[64] In doing this, we prioritize the social media connection as part of journalists' labor, a form of labor that is emerging and developing within the profession and that is largely unsupported by employers; thus, it creates impacts that journalists have so far been individually negotiating through forms of disconnection.

In this chapter, we have defined and conceptualized the forms of connection and disconnection that journalists negotiate in social media environments. Using the lived experiences of journalists, especially during the ongoing COVID-19 pandemic, has shown the paradoxical nature of connection on social media. On the one hand, the public service role of journalism and the relationships journalists have with their audiences have never been so important. Yet journalists all over the world have described the negative impacts of this connection: the relentlessness of social media work in a context of risk, precarity, and physical and mental harm. These risks have become even more prominent as issues external to journalism, such as platform ownership and the impact on how journalists produce news and how audiences consume it. The recent purchase of Twitter by billionaire Elon Musk, for example, indicates how quickly media workers of all kinds must adjust to the changing social, political, and economic landscapes of online interactions.

In the context of journalism and social media work, disconnection often focuses on mitigating or responding to work-related burnout after prolonged social media use. While journalists have been encouraged to change labor practices to be more connected and engaged with audiences, there are many organizational, social, and political contexts that encourage forms of disconnection to maintain and facilitate continued connectivity. Practices of connection and disconnection afford users options, and journalists can attempt to strengthen connections by selectively aiming to control presence while they also foster safer spaces for connection.

This context provides the framework for the remainder of this book to explore the strategies, activities, and decisions that journalists make to negotiate social media use in their everyday work. We show that journalists negotiate uses of social media constantly and according to different influences, including professional needs, traditional boundaries of professional identity and ideologies, structural inequalities, and the necessity of living and working productively within the limitations of digital labor. In the next chapter, we explore the forms of disconnection journalists engage to protect themselves from the personal and professional impacts of ongoing social media use.

CHAPTER 2

Burning Out, Turning Off, and Disconnecting

As the lead journalist on ABC Australia's rural news program, *Landline*, Pip Courtney is constantly on the road, traveling enormous distances across the country to report on the politics of agriculture, farming, and the environment. But even when she finds herself in the farthest reaches of rural Australia, she is always connected to social media. When she first began using social media, she said she tried to post "straight-up journalism" and was surprised by the lack of online audience reaction and engagement with what she saw as important rural news.[1] Courtney quickly realized that to maintain a connection with the loyal *Landline* audience, she had to give them something else: her own life as a journalist. She said she started to post images of her life on the road: playing with cute farm animals, getting lost on long stretches of outback road, and being the victim of the practical jokes played on her by her camera crew. She slowly built a loyal online community by continually posting about her professional life as a journalist, with followers responding to her by commenting on the television program or talking about their own issues with life on the land.

By fostering online connections based on discussion of her professional life, Courtney said that in addition to the *Landline* television audience, she now has a strong, global online following whose members have never actually watched the television program she hosts: "I've actually got some good Twitter mates. People I've never met, but we have good conversations on Twitter. I feel like I've got a little army of friends I've never met out there." While Courtney enjoys these interactions as part of her professional life, fostering these connections is still a form of affective labor. Courtney might allow her "Twitter mates" a sneak peek behind the scenes of making the *Landline* program, but there is no doubt that their connection is based on shared interest in her area of reportage. Accordingly, she never lets them into her personal life or online spaces. Her decisions about how to post were the result of negative interactions on social media. "I used to get quite distressed with some of the toxic conversations. But I just realized, you've got to block, you've got to mute. You've got to protect your home and your environment from certain people."

The demarcation between professional and private relations that Courtney is referring to has not always been foregrounded in journalistic use of social media. While media organizations were initially slow to incorporate social media into journalism, research shows that they are now actively encouraging journalists like Courtney to engage with existing and potential audiences using social media.[2] Two things have happened as a result: first, social media users tend to follow individual journalists much more than they do news organizations, and second, journalists are feeling increasing pressure to be the popular face of their news organizations on social media.

Much of the initial research around newsroom integration of social media shows that social media policy has tended toward more general guidelines around what those online interactions should comprise.[3] As a result, journalists have developed individual strategies around what they share online. As shown in chapter 1, many of these strategies are based on fostering and maintaining forms of connection with social media followers for different organizational and professional needs. However, negative online experiences, such as reputational damage around online errors, increased labor expectations, trolling, and harassment, can also influence journalists' social media strategies.

In chapter 1, we suggested that increasing professionalization of social media platforms has encouraged journalists and news organizations to devote more labor toward online audience engagement, whether it relates to marketing practices of newsrooms, the consumption patterns of audiences, or the more civic practices of online collaboration. While these strategies present opportunities for journalists to develop online reportage practices, this feeling of always being connected also impacts the journalists themselves. This chapter focuses attention on an aspect of social media labor among professional journalists: the disconnection strategies they use to establish professional and personal boundaries in social media use.

Drawing on over thirty semistructured interviews conducted with professional journalists in Australia and the United States working in print and broadcast and online, this chapter outlines the obstacles journalists encountered when they posted professional content and what impact this had on their use of social media. News organizations are also increasingly encouraging adoption of promotion and engagement practices on both organizational and personal social media profiles. As a result, journalists increasingly reported that the labor required to engage in social media practices and the complex literacies required to understand social expectations in these spaces are leading to more negative experiences online.[4]

We found that several issues emerged, including perceptions of professional work seeping into journalists' personal lives and anxiety about the reputational risk that social media politics, etiquettes, and cultures brought to their professional lives. Journalists have also suggested fear of professional or personal repercussions from erroneous or controversial posting. For example, the Australian ABC journalist Louise Milligan was successfully sued for defamation by the federal MP Andrew Laming over four tweets, totaling approximately $130,000 in damages.[5] These issues also led some journalists to describe feelings of mental and physical burnout. Burnout refers to many issues, including frustration with perception of increased affective labor, dissatisfaction with communication cultures on specific social media platforms, and increased anxiety about the impact of social media use on mental and physical well-being.[6]

Protecting themselves against these impacts subsequently led to journalists' use of disconnection strategies, including reducing personal posting and interactions with unknown users, changing the kinds of content posted, and occasionally "switching off" from social media altogether. Disconnection strategies are the purposeful disengagement activities that individuals use to avoid or mediate the connective affordances of particular social media platforms. As suggested in chapter 1, disconnection strategies can include creating private spheres for interaction, using technical boundaries like blocking and muting, and turning away from interaction altogether. Tero Karppi suggests that leaving social media platforms altogether for extended periods of time is also an important aspect of mediating and finding value in connectivity that comes with both rewards, such as less anxiety about constant connection, and risks, such as increased isolation.[7]

Previous research on forms of disconnection suggests that most users, including journalists, have a clear reason for disconnection and have put these strategies into place after some reflection. Journalists' reasons may include political or ideological resistance to particular social media affordances, protection from personal or professional harms, and improving online privacy.[8] In this context, disconnection strategies are an important part of journalistic labor because they allow for negotiation of the emerging practices, organizational routines, and perceptions of work and life balance within journalists' own professional and personal online identities.

Online Journalism Practices and Burnout

Workers in many professions have been impacted by cultures of sharing on social media.[9] Much of the focus of these new forms of labor has been on the creative and informational content available through online and social media.[10] These forms of labor are defined by immateriality, that is, the creation and networked distribution of symbolic, informational, or affective products and services.[11] The impact of these new forms of labor is complex. While some understand "immaterial labor" as the deepening of organizational jurisdiction into everyday life, Tiziana Terranova suggests that affective and often "free labor . . . is not necessarily exploited labor" but rather a form of agreed exchange within networked publics with complicated impacts.[12] These exchanges are labor, but they can also be seen in the context of building and engaging with the community, being creative, expanding personal and professional networks, and engaging in pleasurable activities. This increasing personalization of an individual's relationship to labor, not just in journalism but more broadly, has led to increased blurring of professional practices within otherwise personal spaces.

Continual development of strategies to incorporate online practices into traditional news work has led to what many journalists describe as an imbalance in their work and personal lives, including feelings of burnout. Christina Maslach and Susan Jackson describe professional burnout as feelings of emotional exhaustion created by a stressful work environment and characterized by cynical attitudes toward work, sensitivity to professional feedback, and dissatisfaction with professional accomplishments.[13]

Research about burnout in journalism often examines the impact of specific forms of reportage, such as emergency and conflict reportage, as well as stressful newsroom environments.[14] The symptoms include increased self-reported levels of exhaustion, cynicism about one's role, and perceptions of decreased professional efficacy. Research conducted in non-Western contexts has also described the physical danger journalists face by incorporating online work into news routines due to political sensitivity around sharing information. Journalists reporting on cartel violence in northern Mexico have not been able to freely share information online, instead using social media to circumvent the security risks of their work.[15]

Much research around burnout describes the physicality of overwork: the ramifications for the body of a stressful work environment. We propose that feelings of burnout on social media are not just physical. Rather, feelings of burnout can also stem from the complexity of incorporating new practices and professional norms into everyday labor, such as learning the new vernacular, practices, and literacies of social media. Scott Reinardy suggests that this working environment has created symptoms of burnout, particularly among early career journalists.[16] Indeed, recent research suggests that younger female journalists and editors in small-circulation newspapers may be most at risk of burnout.[17] Similar research has shown that the financial decline of traditional media has contributed to more pressure on journalists, who must produce good-quality work with fewer staff, on shorter deadlines, and across more platforms, despite overall lower remuneration and promotion opportunities.

How Do Journalists Describe Burnout?

Many of the journalists we interviewed maintained that social media was integral to their work. Most said that social media was a productive addition to their professional practice, particularly promoting their work to a larger audience (see chapter 3). But journalists also described negative impacts stemming mostly from frustration and anxiety around the increased but often unacknowledged affective or relational labor of everyday social media use. The journalists we interviewed expressed frustration and anxiety about the impact of these forms of labor on their personal and professional lives. This continual relational labor had consequences for journalists' well-being. One journalist said, "Social media, when you're a journalist, it's always on. There's always stuff to read, and you're always consuming information. . . . Part of it is recognition that using those spaces too much, for me, is directly related to increasing my anxiety and stress."[18]

Along with describing their anxieties about the constant use of relational labor, journalists also suggested that the types of interactions required created anxiety about what was appropriate to share in these spaces.[19] Part of the frustration that journalists expressed about this type of labor was the pressure to keep up with the social vernacular expected within the often platform-specific communication cultures. Journalists suggested that this labor of keeping up with social media cultures led to professional anxiety about being able to do their job properly. The lack of contextual control journalists have on platforms such as Twitter and the lack of control over audience responses led to this journalist enacting practices that were protective of personal and professional reputation.

Journalists described a "wariness," as well as a "risk-averse" and "sometimes discomforting" experience of social media in their professional lives due to perceived reputational damage that any misuse of platforms might have.

Many of the journalists we interviewed said these experiences had resulted in a careful renegotiation of the professional and personal boundaries of their social media use; in particular, they reported various strategies used to disconnect from or switch off social media in their personal time. Journalists reported instances of self-censoring and profile management, as well as careful negotiation of production and sharing of personal content. One journalist noted, "I think I probably have self-censored on occasion if I had a really strong opinion about something. If I want to express that opinion, I'm better off writing a full story about it and then tweeting the link to that story rather than expressing my opinion in 140 characters and then possibly getting trolled or abused or something."[20]

How Do Journalists Disconnect?

Journalists suggested that disconnection strategies made it possible for them to live with connectivity. For journalists who feel compelled both professionally and organizationally to use social media to connect with potential news audiences, disconnection also encompasses the strategic ways users make social media work according to individual needs.[21] It is disconnection that contributes to the potential of connective affordances on particular social media platforms because it encourages more personalized and workable uses of social media according to individual needs and desires.[22] For journalists using social media as a professional communication tool, disconnection strategies actually work in tandem with the different ways they connect online, positioning those connections more strategically as professional labor and thus inscribing particular meanings and uses for social media interactions.

Ben Light argues that these situated forms of disconnection empower strategic decision-making around online use and thus strengthen subsequent forms of online connection.[23] Modes of disengagement are actively chosen or developed over time to avoid or mediate the connective affordances of particular social media. While disconnection is often thought about as turning off from social media in personal time, this does not necessarily mean ending all social media use. Instead, disconnection is seen as part of an overall strategy developed over time and upon reflection about many different types of personal and professional experiences on social media. For journalists, the importance of disconnection is not simply to stop use of social media but rather to make social media work according to their professional and personal needs.[24]

Experiences and use of disconnection strategies illustrate the operational necessities of social media use within the everyday lived experiences of journalists in a professional context.[25] Disconnection strategies allow journalists to create their own boundaries around labor and leisure online and to create subsequently meaningful engagements with both their online audiences and their personal networks. Individuals might limit social media connectivity to manage large audiences or workload or to maintain a particular self-representation online; however, these disconnection strategies still add value and individual meaning to online experiences.[26]

The interviews we conducted revealed different disconnection strategies associated with avoidance or turning off certain types of connections, such as suspension or avoidance of particular social media profiles; muting, blocking, or using other technical barriers to engagement; and finally, changing the types of interactions that journalists had on social media. The interviews indicated that many of these strategies were the result of journalists' deep reflection about the impact that some social media cultures had on their personal lives and well-being, while others were symptomatic of the development of professionalized social media use.

Journalists also suggested that their introduction of disconnection strategies had to be balanced with organizational policies and editorial guidelines for social media use (see chapter 4 on social media policy). Most often, the disconnection strategies influenced by organizational ideologies were modes of self-censorship, that is, avoiding posting some forms of social media content.[27] A journalist confided: "You'd be crazy to think you could just get away with posting anything. The general sense of it [social media policy] is that you have to be conscious of the reputation of who you work for, and you don't write anything that would be embarrassing or compromising."[28]

While this kind of self-censorship seemed to be influenced by organizational concerns with potential legal issues, other journalists suggested that individual and organizational reputations were factors in censoring social media content. As a journalist suggested, "What we have is sort of a system where our company is our parents, and our colleagues are more like our best friends. We care what our parents think, and we know they can take our allowance away if we don't do what we're told, but it's what our friends think of us that matters most." In this way, individual professional reputation may also be bound up in the reputation of the organization the journalist works for. Both need to be credible in order to adhere to particular professional ideologies; thus, avoiding posting of some content is important in this context.

This response indicates an important aspect of disconnection strategies: the influence that different social contexts and forms of power has on social media practices of connection and disconnection. Journalists differed in response to how acutely aware of organizational policies and pressures they were. Some journalists were aware of branding strategies and the need to keep their social media "assets in line with who [news organizations] want us to be, what they post, and who they want us to engage with." Most journalists ensured that they were posting regularly and with content that aligned with the editorial considerations of the newsroom. A journalist suggested that these pressures were a source of anxiety, as taking a break from social media had been positioned by newsroom management as a dereliction of their professional duties: "Would it be . . . a violation of my journalistic responsibilities by breaking away or ignoring one channel? Would [my news organization] send out a memorandum about it or maybe fire me?" What these different approaches suggest is that connection and disconnection strategies were decisions made by individual journalists, with each considering beliefs, actions, and consequences at the individual, organizational, and institutional levels.

Disconnection from Platforms or Platform-Specific Cultures

Many disconnection strategies were situated not within the workplace but within particular platforms and interactions. Having control over the types of platforms used and the times they would be available for personal and professional online interaction was seen as empowering to journalists who would otherwise feel overwhelmed by the always-on connectivity of social media. Journalists described professional rules of engagement that they used on social media, limiting interactions to those that had a promotional or professional context. Some journalists said they limited comments and conversation online to users whom they knew personally: "If I'm mentioned in a tweet about a story that I've written or if I post a story I've written, or people write back to me or tweet at me about the story, I'll probably generally like a comment. But I don't usually engage in back-and-forth conversation. I'd say I'm a little more inclined to do so when it's like a verified account or it's like a fellow journalist of whom I'm aware."[29] Other strategies included only engaging with other professional journalists, only answering legitimate questions about reportage, or turning off comments altogether. Other journalists had private personal accounts or used profiles with pseudonyms when they used social media in personal time. While many of these rules seemed to be individual techniques of online engagement, they had also been normalized in newsrooms and were passed on to more junior employees or discussed with social media managers.

Journalists used these rules to avoid negative confrontations during their professional use of social media. Women journalists we interviewed suggested that some social media cultures were more "vicious" toward women than others (see chapter 6 for discussion about online harassment). While most forms of trolling are defined as "malicious online behavior, intended to disrupt interactions, aggravate interactional partners and lure them into fruitless argumentation," trolling aimed toward women is generally distinguished by threats of physical and sexual violence and misogynistic abuse.[30] Thus, boundaries around interactions seemed particularly relevant to women, especially those who had experienced these forms of trolling in the past. One woman journalist said they modeled their online interactions on their sense of appropriate offline behavior: "If you wouldn't catch up with them, you wouldn't go out for a coffee with them. If you're in a bar, you would avoid them, so I'm just not going to let them affect my life."[31]

Journalists additionally chose to use boundaries on interaction on a specific platform based on their understanding of its communication culture. Given the extensive journalistic use of Twitter, it was unsurprising that journalists described negative interactions on the platform and the need for limits on forms of connection. One journalist said, "If Twitter were a person, I wouldn't like them. I think that they would just be kind of showy and arrogant and self-bold and snarky, and I'm just not trying to spend time with a person like that."[32]

Suspending participation on specific platforms indicates the situated nature of social media interactions, what Ben Light and Elija Cassidy refer to as the "geographies of disconnection."[33] Journalists we interviewed said they mainly used Twitter and a Facebook page for work-related social media practices but disconnected from these platforms during personal time. They made these decisions based on their perception of the usefulness of the platform for work practice, the perceived culture of the platform itself, and whether specific platforms contributed to poor physical and mental well-being. One journalist said, "I've reduced [social media use] because [of], in general, frustration with the tenor of the conversations in those spaces. Part of that is a desire to be able to switch off more easily. Using those spaces too much, for me, is directly related to increasing my anxiety and stress."[34]

Journalists suggested that feelings of burnout and negative experiences online had influenced their strategies of avoidance of social media in their personal time. A journalist described their development of boundaries over time:

"I actually have found over the years, I think I post a lot less than other people in personal terms. I think because as a journalist, publishing is our whole life, it's what we do. . . . I'm publishing all day long."[35] Others suggested that the protection of personal time was important: "I'm quite a private person, and I like my space. I like my mental space, and I guess, technically, I would always try to use social media toward maintaining privacy."[36] Journalists might choose efficiencies in their management of social media platforms or selectively control their online presence in ways that kept them sane. All these strategies, though they might be seen as a turning away from or a nonuse of social media, are nonetheless crucial because they add specific meaning or value to subsequent or alternative online experiences.

Disconnection by Enacting Personal Social Media Boundaries

Journalists we spoke to suggested that they represented details about their professional lives on their public social media accounts, although they avoided posting personal details about their lives, opinions, or interests.[37] Journalists we interviewed suggested that they chose not to post professional work on any personal profiles and not to share opinions on a professional profile. They therefore engaged in an ethics of disconnection, extending a duty of care toward personal friend networks who might not want their interactions seen by a number of news users and a professional duty of care to audiences following their work on social media who expect the expression of particular professional values. Journalists also suggested that they did this because they were cognizant of organizational pressures to engage in nonrisky behaviors on social media: "It's something that I'm very keenly aware of, that my public posting social media account needs to be more cautious rather than more off-the-cuff and playful and experimental." They also suggested that avoiding anything other than a professional persona online was in keeping with their own professional ideologies around news reportage: "They followed me for a reason, not because they're my friend. They followed me because they're interested in my stories or they're interested in the topics that I'm writing about."[38]

Similar to this adherence to professional ideologies, Light and Cassidy suggest that disconnection strategies can follow an "ethical logic."[39] Although Light has previously suggested that privacy is perhaps the most obvious reason for engaging disconnection practices, other considerations, such as respect for perceived audiences or followers, perceived relevance of professional or personal posting, and issues of overall health and wellness, might influence a journalist's choices about how to connect.[40]

For professional journalists, ethical decision-making around social media use is made through a lens of professional identity and ideologies. Journalists indicated that their disconnection strategies had developed over time and with their increased experience with social media. For instance, journalists related instances of reflection after a long period of professional use of social media; they were thinking more carefully about how they wanted to use the tool, as well as the personal and professional ethics of connection on social media. While some journalists suggested that this was an outcome of "getting older," we found that similar disconnection strategies were also enacted by less senior journalists, suggesting that individual reflection rather than age or technical ability engendered use of disconnection strategies.

Similarly, Monika Djerf-Pierre, Marina Ghersetti, and Ulrika Hedman suggested that among journalists in Sweden, social media use is continually changing over time.[41] They found that initial adoption of social media was high as journalists trialed the features of specific platforms and then leveled out and normalized as journalists reflected upon the advantages and limitations.[42] Journalists alluded to their ability to negotiate uses of communication technologies, influenced by their personal and professional contexts. In this way, journalists' disconnection strategies may be seen as a series of options negotiated and influenced through individual conditions of use of social media, which are framed by a platform's particular affordances and materiality and by the boundaries of a journalist's organizational and institutional framework.

This chapter illustrated some of the frameworks for use of disconnection by journalists navigating professional labor on social media, including negotiating the technical and social affordances of platforms. While modes of connection have brought many opportunities to improve journalistic practices online, this book foregrounds that these professionalized social media practices have also had material impacts on journalists and their work. This chapter has shown how important context-specific and individualized strategies of disconnection are to journalists needing to create workable boundaries in order to function within the always-on connectivity of social media.

Journalists enact disconnection not only within the workplace but also within different platforms and interactions or between personal and professional self-representation online. These strategies were associated with the avoidance of online connections, including not using particular social media profiles; suspending specific platforms; muting, blocking, or forming other technical barriers to engagement; or changing the types of interactions on platforms. The interviews indicated that many of these strategies were the result of either negative experiences with particular social media platforms or the continual development of a more professional interaction with platforms based on the journalists' own reflection about the impact that use of social media cultures had on their personal lives.

Journalists adopt social media cultures that prioritize openness and collaboration with audiences. These cultures in turn challenge the way traditional practices are valued in this space. However, with the integration of these practices and cultures come different impacts not just on the news organizations and the profession but also on the journalists themselves. By developing strategies of both connection and disconnection, journalists can manage the transition to forms of news production, distribution, and engagement enabled by online and social media.

In this chapter, we also illustrated that disconnection does not mean termination of professional connection online. While connection and disconnection practices are the result of the active negotiation of empowered online users, these practices are also influenced by the technological, social, and cultural affordances of specific media platforms, as well as the online literacies and behaviors of the users themselves. Indeed, many of the issues journalists faced when using social media in their practice were necessarily productive; they highlight how journalism, like all communication practices, must reflect on and respond to technological changes and to the social and cultural changes that emerge alongside them. Thus, it is not necessarily the expertise or skill of the journalist that is being renegotiated in social media environments nor the need for professional journalism overall. The transition in journalistic practices is due to the changing relations between journalists and their audiences, their organizations, their professional identity, and, thus, their changing role in social life.

In chapter 3 we focus on one aspect of journalists' negotiation of social media work, that is, use of personal and professional branding as an aspect of professional identity construction and audience connection online. Branding strategies maintain a particular type of connection with audiences, but journalists also navigate tensions between personal disclosure for authenticity and professional credibility and between establishing individual distinctiveness and promoting an employer. We conceptualize how professional branding on social media has been used by journalists grappling with online economies of authenticity and attention.

PART II

Connection and Disconnection in Organizational Contexts

CHAPTER 3

Maintaining Professional Connections through Branding

Substack, a newsletter platform that helps writers publish and distribute their work through a tiered subscription system, has poached several top figures in journalism since 2020. The newsletter platform presents a mix of "career journalists, bloggers, specialists, novelists, hobbyists, dabblers, and white-collar professionals looking to plump up their personal brand," enhance their individual visibility, and make an income.[1] Indeed, it has become a viable source of revenue for many writers. Several journalists, dubbed the "Substackerati," have turned to the subscription platform for financial and resource security.[2] Casey Newton, formerly of *The Verge*, said working with Substack meant accessing additional healthcare and the promise of a million-dollar legal defense fund.[3] Journalists are also promised the ability to control their email lists, archives, and intellectual property. While these benefits may have wide appeal, they are only within reach for those journalists who publicize their brand and content enough to build a following that is willing to pay.[4]

Substack represents one of the key digital labor paradoxes journalists face: the more news organizations push journalists to be on social media, the greater the likelihood they will realize enough success to strike out on their own. Some journalists have reported moving to Substack in part because of their exhaustion from the content pressure of the news media industry. Substack enables journalists to set their own timelines. Others have suggested that the additional labor of practicing journalism on social media could be used more entrepreneurially.[5] Newton suggested in an interview that ongoing digital disruption has meant not only increased precarity but also more risk-taking on the part of journalists looking to channel their skills into more sustainable media business models.[6] However, other research has found that the subscription-based economic models influencing modern journalism often reproduce the same entrepreneurial precarity and other professional issues plaguing the media industry, such as lack of diversity and gatekeeping.[7] Further, we know little about how relationships between journalists and their audience may evolve on this platform, raising questions about whether they may produce the same antagonistic and abusive communication environments that pushed some journalists to leave their former publications in the first place. Substack's model may work well for writers who already have a large social following, but it also highlights the gaps in entrepreneurial logics around personal and professional branding on social media.

Self-branding practices demonstrate the paradoxical complexities of working on social media. After all, many journalists who use Substack find themselves part of a gig economy in which they have to take other jobs in order to make ends meet. As Clio Chang points out, journalists on the newsletter platform must continue to promote their work distinctively through social media, which can be exhausting and even lead to burnout.[8] Personal branding is, after all, a form of labor that prioritizes connection through personality branding and affective relationships with users while also navigating different platform cultures and their vernaculars, on top of navigating unclear and often changing newsroom policies about using social media.[9]

In this chapter we turn to some of the paradoxes of connecting with diverse audiences via personal branding on social media. In the previous chapter, we discussed the disconnection strategies used by journalists to mediate some of the complexities of social media spaces. Now we take a step back into the modes of connection journalists have used to engage audiences online and the inherent paradoxes within them. The emergence of social media has assisted in creating seemingly unbounded spaces for user participation where audiences are able to critique, re-present, dismiss, or simply ignore the journalist. Many have hoped that these interactions would approach an ideal of participatory communication as people engage issues and debate collaboratively within networks to effect change.[10] The reality is instead a fight for attention as journalists join throngs of influencers and celebrities on social media, each clamoring for an audience.

We focus on the origins of journalistic social media branding practices amid labor market precarity, platformization, and several crises in journalism. Employers and journalists alike have realized the entrepreneurial potential of social media in journalism, but these commercialized logics have created some paradoxical impacts, including labor precarity, increased affective labor, and burnout. We discuss how branding is practiced among journalists before turning to the many tensions it creates. This chapter concludes with discussions of the normative issues inherent in journalistic branding and the ways this practice provides a contextual framework for journalists' use of disconnection strategies.

The Origins of Personal Branding in Media Work

Concern for reputation is now a characteristic of working lives driven in part by modern professionalization values that prioritize image and status.[11] The idea that workers must create and maintain individually recognizable professional personas is a relatively recent development, and while it is not shared by all cultures, it has nonetheless become a feature of Western, modern-industrial life. While the forces that led to the rise of personal branding have been decades in the making, the popularization of the term "personal brand" is often credited to a 1997 article in the business magazine *Fast Company*.[12]

Branding in the case of large organizations is about distinguishing a product or service from competitors and making promises about its originality and quality.[13] Branding work generally takes the form of an organized campaign carried out over time and usually on various media channels in order to establish a relationship with consumers and gain their loyalty.[14] The campaign seeks a particular audience and crafts messages that encourage economic and emotional commitment to the object being branded.[15] In short, these communications seek to influence future transactions and build the organization's reputation.

Personal branding adapts the above ideas to individual workers, establishing the person as a professional entity and making assertions about their goals, experience, traits, and capabilities. Employees, having once made this case to an employer to be hired, were not generally motivated to devote attention to their personal brand until it was time to seek a new job. There are longtime exceptions, such as salespeople, whose work depends upon transactions negotiated in person and commission-based payment. But in most cases, rank-and-file employees had little reason to be seen or known by those consuming their firm's product or services.

Over the past decades, this situation has changed, most notably for media and other knowledge workers, as part of larger neoliberal trends in the global labor market.[16] Technology, including social media, is central in these trends, giving firms access to both new markets and new sources of labor and placing more firms in competition with each other. For media industries, digital disruption has been devastating to traditional media businesses, with smaller, local, and print-only media seeing devastating cuts in revenue. Unions have also continued to decline over the past half century, weakening the primary form of organization and advocacy on behalf of workers. In the United States especially, there has been an ideological shift toward individualism and personal responsibility that is reflected in government policies weakening regulation of firms and removing protections for workers.[17] Arne Kalleberg views this shift as the action of a pendulum swinging between heavily regulated markets that lead businesses to demand more flexibility and free and flexible markets that leave workers clamoring for greater security.

Branding as a Response to Crisis

Media workers around the world are responding to a precarious labor market and the rise of platforms by adopting practices of personal branding on social media. Indeed, branding can be seen as a response to several crises that have beset the media industry and, by extension, journalistic practice. First, eroded institutional support has increased precarity in the job market, leading many journalists to strike out on their own. Second, trust in journalism has continued to fall in some countries, fueled in part by a rise of populist politics in Western democracies, a decline that many journalists reason might be addressed by the increased transparency that branding practices offer. Third, journalism in general and individual news organizations specifically are grappling with fragmentation of the audience, increasing the need for online branding as a means of attracting attention to their work. Each of these challenges has been characterized as a crisis—of economics, of trust, and of attention.

Part of the reason that media workers are so acutely affected by general changes in the labor market is that the firms they work for have been significantly weakened in the last twenty years. Since 2008 the industry as a whole has lost a quarter of its workforce; newspaper employment has been cut in half.[18] The revenue picture is mixed, with television advertising dollars following familiar election cycles but still losing billions in revenue each year to digital media giants.[19] US newspapers, however, had already lost two-thirds of their revenue over a twelve-year stretch before the coronavirus pandemic began, and it only got worse from there.[20] This is a particularly troubling statistic, given that newspapers still produce a large majority of the local news in US communities.[21] This is not a uniquely American crisis—a global survey found that advertising revenue decline is one of the biggest threats facing the news industry.[22] The situation is not much brighter in Europe despite a tradition of publicly funded news media.

The global media industry has adopted precarity as a labor response to plummeting advertising revenue and the rise of digital advertising technologies on social media. Precarity is defined as work that is "uncertain, unpredictable and risky from the point of view of the worker."[23] Jeremias Prassl supports this assessment of the US labor market with evidence of declining job tenure, increasing long-term unemployment, increasing perceptions of job insecurity, and the growth of nonstandard work arrangements and contingent work, often referred to as the "gig economy."[24] All of this has come along with a cultural valorization of entrepreneurs and entrepreneurship as a form of work, ironically leading workers to blame their precarity on themselves rather than on the decisions of firms or governments. Workers respond by seeking security and a stable sense of self at work through practices of branding, thereby also increasing their value to the firm without additional compensation for it.[25] Rather than viewing this as exploitation, many workers see it as an investment in themselves that will be paid off with a greater reputation, independence, and flexibility.[26] Different market conditions and regulatory practices in other countries have managed these circumstances in different ways, but there is a global trend toward precarity among knowledge workers generally and media workers specifically.[27] When the organizations journalists work for are weakened—economically, through government policy, or otherwise—journalists themselves bear more of the responsibility for the stability that employment provides, leading them toward personal branding as a practice.

Market conditions, coupled with the rise of high-choice media environments, have led many consumers to exercise preference for entertainment over news.[28] Data gathered by the Pew Research center show that newspaper circulations have dropped precipitously, whereas television audiences are flat in recent years. Digital news audiences continue to grow but still represent only a portion of overall news reach. The rise of search engines and of social media networks has added another layer of separation between news organizations and their audiences, such that substantial portions of consumers now encounter news only through those avenues rather than visiting a news organization's website. This has led to a widespread feeling that "the news finds me" or that news exposure is largely incidental rather than intentional.[29] Overall, these developments have meant that journalists have had to compete for audiences and to bear some responsibility for attracting them in the first place.[30]

Personal branding is one of the key tactics here, adopting commercialization and marketing practices for the purpose of attracting attention to one's own work or the work of one's colleagues. The rise of personal branding has also been aided by the widespread adoption and popularization of social media. Social media networks are understood as spaces driven by use of affect, emotion, and performance of authenticity, emphasizing the importance of personal connection, image, and reputation.[31] One of the key innovations of social media has been to quantify this reputation through metrics such as likes, favorites, followers, and so on, allowing users to see their own contributions to the network alongside those of others. Making reputations tangible is a large part of what makes these networks such powerful vehicles of reputation management.[32] Furthermore, especially in the case of freelancers and entrepreneurs, reputation directly impacts one's job prospects. But providing visible measures of reputation also causes creators to try to reverse-engineer content and actions on the platform to bring the greatest visibility.[33] This is emblematic of the ways creative workers are beholden to the platforms they rely upon for visibility, because they must adapt their practices to platforms and their technical and cultural affordances. This means that creative workers are subject to precarity not only in the general labor market and in the industries where they specialize but also on the platforms they use to build their reputations, creating "nested precarities of visibility."[34] As platforms are the infrastructure upon which modern creative work is built, creative workers such as journalists are under increasing professional and organizational pressure to gain visibility for themselves and their work online.[35] Meanwhile, the affordances of and changes in these platforms substantially inform who gains and loses reputation there, leaving journalists somewhat at their mercy.

Social Media Branding in Practice

Increasing job uncertainty and reliance on online tools for everyday work have fostered an environment where personal branding practices thrive among journalists. Journalists interviewed about using social media for personal branding reported that they saw it as a necessary, unavoidable part of the job.[36] A later survey of journalists asked them to identify the source of pressures to practice branding, and many replied that source was themselves or their own sense of market or environmental pressures favoring those with a personal brand.[37] Journalists typically focus their branding efforts on three targets: the individual, the organization, and the institution of journalism. Individual branding may be either personal or professional, whereas both organizational and institutional branding practices have a primarily professional focus.

Individual journalists often practice personal branding by promoting themselves. That is, beyond being a messenger of news and current events, journalists use social media to speak about themselves, their lives, and their work as a form of individual journalistic branding. While individual branding is most often focused on identity and role performance, branding practices have taken on a number of formats, from fully promotional practices to more relational practices that help to build community around particular issues and journalists.[38] Previous research has shown that professional identity branding is a typical journalistic use of social media that identifies specific branding practices, such as the use of humor, audience engagement with marketing and media consumption, and personal information.[39] However, other research has shown that the content and purpose of promotional posts were often framed to correspond with how an individual journalist believed their professional role should be articulated within a particular social media platform culture and its affordances. For some journalists, this might mean using and normalizing common forms of online professional branding such as sharing one's work or media appearances, but for others this might mean using affective or relational labor or even an "aspirational aesthetic" more commonly attributed to online influencers.[40]

Journalists also promote their colleagues and the news organizations they work for through organizational branding. Journalists use platform affordances such as tagging, hash tagging, and linking to promote their colleagues' work, or they may interact with them directly through commenting on or sharing their work. Some journalists suggest that they do this more organizationally focused branding work as a form of digital sourcing or citing of news, while others seek to engage audiences in these more professionally focused conversations about news. To this end, journalists also use social media practices that speak about journalism in general, which constitutes institutional branding, though this is rarer. What is more common is that many of these types of branding are expressed in representational practices that differ according to the perceived culture of the platform, the type of journalism being practiced, and even a journalist's own professional and personal satisfaction in using particular social media practices. Many of these practices have been studied through interviews with journalists, qualitative textual analysis, quantitative content analysis, and surveys of journalists.[41] This section summarizes these findings with an eye toward identifying consistent patterns in journalistic branding practice.

The social media profile is core to branding practices. The profile invites the user to create a name or handle, provide a short bio or description, and post images or links that help to define the profile. All of this information contributes to the user's presence online, and because it is provided by the user it has been said that people are able to type themselves into being.[42] Journalists most frequently mention their employer affiliation and coverage area, and they provide personal information about themselves. Less frequently, journalists mention other news organizations and journalists, or they place disclaimers ("opinions my own") in their bios. Beyond the bio, some journalists mention their employer in their social media handle itself ("@AshleyBK_KVUE").

Journalists use images to build their brand in social media profiles.[43] The main profile image is most often a headshot of a person making eye contact with the camera and smiling. A small portion of these images are selfies, and most people are depicted in professional dress, suggesting the overall professional orientation of profile images. Journalists also use a wide range of other images (such as a header image on the profile page) to depict themselves at work or to depict a location. Taken together, this effort to describe oneself in a social media profile using text and images is a primary form of journalistic branding.

Journalists use their social media posts to further enhance their brand. This has most commonly been observed in journalists' use of Twitter, but studies of other platforms have found similar trends.[44] In their posts, journalists speak about themselves by mentioning experiences they have had, describing what they are doing, or pointing to their recently completed or upcoming work. These individual branding practices serve to promote a journalist's work while also allowing them to present themselves as they would like to be known to their audiences. This shows that most journalists have accepted and incorporated some of the blurred boundaries between professional and personal content into their everyday posting practices.

Journalists also mention their employer or their coworkers, usually by linking to or mentioning work done by their colleagues. As surveys and interviews have shown, this is a response to organizational mandates to represent the company and help further the news organization's brand. Finally, mentions of other journalists or of journalism in general—known as institutional branding—were less common but still sought to express solidarity or build up the profession as a whole in the face of dwindling trust.

Not all journalists perform these branding practices in the same way. Gender plays an important role in how journalists present themselves, with women overall presenting a more personalized self-image than men. In other words, women journalists are more likely to consider individual elements of branding important and include more personal information in their posts and bios. Women more often use profile images that evoke interpersonal exchange, such as eye contact or smiling. Men, on the other hand, are more likely to speak about work and their coverage area and to use photos of themselves at work.[45]

Branding enactment also varies by age (or tenure on the job), size of the news organization, and news beat. Younger journalists take a more individual approach, whereas older journalists tend to adhere closely to the organization and promote it while giving less attention to personal brands. A likely explanation for this is that attachment to an employer grows over time and that younger journalists are more affected by increasing precarity in the job market. Branding practices also vary by the size of the news organization. Those at smaller news organizations felt more free to take an individual approach compared with those at larger news organizations, which presumably have more corporate oversight and hence more developed policies. Branding practice also varies by beat, with those covering politics and public affairs somewhat less likely to engage in personal branding compared with reporters in sports and lifestyle coverage. Finally, platform affordances can shape the forms of branding practices, being more image-heavy on Instagram and more text-heavy on Twitter, for example.[46]

Taken together, these studies provide a body of evidence that journalists spend a substantial amount of their social media messaging on branding activities as opposed to a strict diet of news alerts. Journalists regularly speak about themselves, their work, their colleagues, their organizations, and journalism, all in an effort to shape the images and reputations their audiences perceive. These practices may seem relatively benign and even contextually appropriate on social media, but the reality is that they challenge journalistic norms and create tensions in journalists' everyday work. Adopting branding practices has caused journalists to question what is important in their work and where their attention should focus, creating questions of identity that complicate practices for journalists and their employers alike.

Tensions in Maintaining Connection through Branding

While many branding practices are commonplace within journalists' everyday use of social media, some tensions arise as journalists navigate uncertain and evolving territory. The most prominent of these tensions exist between the personal and professional, pitting traditional media logics against newer social media logics and between the individual and organizational, redistributing employees' power and autonomy. The multiplicity of practices and personas required to present oneself to various audiences across multiple platforms creates a number of tensions in journalistic practice. At the heart of these tensions are questions of identity, including which identities to adopt and how best to present them online.

A key point in understanding the role of identity as a concept in branding is that the creation and maintenance of an identity involve distinguishing the self from others.[47] That is, drawing lines that separate an individual from others or that indicate where the self ends is part of defining an identity. Without that separation, the self is indistinguishable from others. This concept is often discussed as autonomy, especially in literature related to the workplace.[48] The more autonomy an individual has—to make their own decisions and oversee their own work—the greater their sense of identity. This is important because the tensions examined here arise when journalists are asked to balance competing priorities and approaches to online communication. To the extent that they can navigate these challenges autonomously, journalists report fulfillment in shaping their own identities; conversely, those who feel that policy or other pressures force their hand report a stifling loss of their sense of self.[49]

This tension in identity is most salient for journalists along what has been described as a spectrum between the personal and the professional.[50] On the one hand, traditional media logics have held that journalists need no public-facing persona or that when one does exist, it is primarily a professional one focused on their role as a journalist. This is evident in news networks' efforts to build up news anchors and other on-air personalities based not on their background or personal interests but on their professionalism and work. This has been seen in social media profiles that are linked specifically to the journalists' news organization; their profile name may include the name of the organization they work for, and even "behind-the-scenes" content is linked specifically to their professional work. Australian television journalists often post images of themselves sitting behind the news desk as a promotion of their upcoming news bulletin.

On the other hand, social media has its own set of logics and culture that encourage journalists to use different posting behaviors. Social networks were of course not designed specifically for journalists, so journalists began to adopt and mediate some of the vernacular practices associated with specific platforms.[51] Among them is a tendency toward personal disclosure, such as information about family life and hobbies.[52] Theresa Senft suggests that more intimate and relatable disclosure and self-presentation practices are created to appear authentic, though they are more likely to be strategic and curated to engage potential followers and improve online popularity. Similarly, use of microcelebrity refers not only to popular social media users but also to the capacity for attention garnered by individual social media users who brand or commodify their unique online personas.[53]

To fit in and to build reputation on these platforms, journalists have had to employ the cultural vernacular of particular platforms and mediate them within journalistic practice. Some research has shown increased uses of aspirational posting, especially by lifestyle journalists on social media. Journalists posting aesthetically pleasing and aspirational content on social media are attempting to maintain a particular online persona to optimize engagement with followers who enjoy the glamour portrayed by journalists, even if those followers don't always engage with those journalists.[54]

The documentation of this glamorous "everyday life" is coupled with strategies that improve journalists' "findability" online, including using popular hashtags, tagging popular people and brands, and commenting on other popular sites to bring audiences to their professional work. Other research has shown that this type of posting relates more to the service provider and recommendation role of the journalist rather than to the public service role, which requires professional distance and objectivity.[55] Within this service provider role, remaining "real" and authentic to and thus trusted by an online community is especially important, even if this community knows that this affective labor is being leveraged as promotion for other news content.[56]

These competing norms and practices have created a tension for journalists: If their feed is too professional, they risk losing audiences who came to social media looking for personal connections. If their feed is too personal, they risk losing a sense of professional reputation or, even worse, facing a reprimand from brand-conscious employers. Journalists and other media workers repeatedly report struggling to find the right balance between personal and professional branding activities.[57] This tension creates a layer of cognitive overhead and emotional labor that complicates journalists' social media use and leads them toward varying levels of connection and disconnection.

Within the more professional side of social media activity, journalists face another layer of tension between their individual brand and that of their organizations. For freelance journalists, this is an obvious choice. The absence of any organizational affiliation leaves them free to focus on developing an individual brand. It is partially for this reason that many studies of personal branding focus on freelance journalists.[58] Journalists employed by an organization, however, must grapple with the extent to which they brand the organization or themselves as separate from it.

Older journalists and those with longer tenure in the industry report a greater allegiance to organizational brands, whereas younger and less experienced journalists prefer an individual branding approach.[59] Women journalists, perhaps underserved by the organizations they work for, also tend to take an individualized (and more personal) approach to branding.[60] Newer research also shows tendencies toward more platform-specific practices by digital-only journalists, such as using selfies on Instagram and a sarcastic or informal tone on Twitter. Nonetheless, this tension between individual and organizational use of branding reflects the dynamic nature of trends in social media practice.

Regardless of age and gender, however, journalists seem to choose one approach or another, aligning their motivations and practices to that approach. This choice has profound ramifications for both the individuals and the organizations at stake. A successfully implemented individual brand can propel a journalist into what is now a booming subscription newsletter business such as Substack, potentially fending off some of the precarity journalists face. The organization, however, stands to lose not only one of their workers but also part of its reputation, which of course is built on the work of its employees. Chapter 5 discusses the ways in which organizational policies have developed in order to safeguard both human and reputational resources in ways that favor the organization.

Like other social media users, journalists deal with context collapse, which occurs when they must consider whom they are speaking to when they post.[61] Journalists' particular form of context collapse is complicated, however, because they operate in a multisided market. That is, speaking only about their professional obligations, journalists must present themselves to three entities who pay for news: audiences, who consume news and purchase subscriptions; employers, who pay for journalists' work; and advertisers, who still provide the majority of funding available to most large news organizations. Journalists run the risk of offending one or more of these economic interests anytime they tweet, a fact that carries no small weight in their considerations.[62]

Beyond this, the fact that journalism is professionalized but not a profession (with exams and licensing, etc.) means that journalists often have no way of knowing whether they are doing their jobs properly other than to compare themselves to their peers.[63] They seek this social validation constantly, and in fact, studies have found that journalists interact primarily with other journalists on Twitter.[64] These interactions are complicated when there are new entrants to the field, including highly partisan actors who embrace different norms.[65]

Journalists must also tailor their messages and approach to different platforms.[66] Twitter's highly textual format encourages certain kinds of content, while Instagram's highly visual format allows others to thrive. Facebook, Snapchat, and now TikTok all have particular cultures and rules of engagement. WhatsApp specializes in one-to-one and small-group communications, requiring still another approach.

Altogether, this variability in audiences and approaches in branding may be referred to as multiplicity, signaling the multiple identities that journalists perform as they practice personal branding. The range of this multiplicity is wider for journalists, perhaps, than for other professionals not working in multisided markets with multiple constituencies. But another striking fact of this multiplicity is that it is malleable, meaning that its forms and enactments are fluid depending on shifting terrain.[67] The risk of reprisal from an offending social media post increases as multiplicity increases, requiring journalists to try on and perform multiple identities as they seek to appease varied audiences.

Branding and Journalism's Normative Values

The proliferation of personal branding as a journalistic practice has called into question several journalistic values. These normative questions are not necessarily paradoxes, but they do illustrate that there are always trade-offs as journalists weigh the adoption of new practices that were originally exogenous to the profession. Because branding requires journalists to concern themselves with the vagaries of platforms and audiences, it challenges the journalistic norm of independence, with consequences for news judgment. Branding as a whole, of course, is an entrepreneurial venture, which is something that has not traditionally been a role individual journalists perform, outside of freelancing. This new form of commercialization may in some ways be preferable to older forms, but one thing it certainly does is shift responsibility toward individual journalists. This shift is almost certain to carry consequences for other aspects of journalistic work as it displaces and subsumes them.

The journalistic norm of independence is generally defined as an independence from any faction or an independence of mind.[68] That is, journalists should seek truth and report it without much regard for whom it pleases or displeases. They should feel free to choose which stories and sources to pursue. But when some portion of journalists' success is measured by the number of people they reach or retain, this desire to please an audience may overwhelm other news judgment instincts. That is, controversial or potentially sensitive story subjects may be avoided for fear of offending social media constituencies. Studies have shown some evidence that audience preferences inform editorial decisions, which of course could be inevitable when audience consumption is crucial to the business model.[69]

But branding raises two additional concerns. First, a susceptibility to audience preferences could now be pushed down to the level of individual journalists rather than resting with a senior editor. Diffusing this pressure only makes it more likely that audience preferences will weigh more heavily in editorial calculations. Second, in cases where perceived audience preferences (or potential damage to a journalist's image) come into conflict with journalism's democratic mission, how will individual journalists decide which impulses to follow? The problem here is that these editorial decisions become infused with personal risk when one's professional (and, to some extent, personal) reputation is also on the line via exposure on social media. News organizations have shown a reluctance to shelter journalists from this risk and instead regularly jettison employees who run afoul of online audiences. Shouldering this risk individually compromises journalists' ability to operate independently.

Some journalists choose a more entrepreneurial route through freelancing or starting their own ventures. However, the emphasis on personal branding also calls into question the desirability and feasibility of turning the field into an array of independent contractors while also expecting them to uphold the mission of an institutionalized press in democracies.[70] Criticisms have already emerged that the path to Substack success is possible for only a select few. It requires a relatively large, stable following in a niche area, combined with cultivation of the intent to pay for this information. Suggesting that all journalists adopt an entrepreneurial stance may deliver a few stars but is unlikely to support the kind of sustained information gathering and dissemination that democracy has traditionally relied on journalists to carry out. That hasn't stopped journalism schools and industry observers from advancing an entrepreneurial ethos that reveres technology.[71] This narrative is most prominent in the United States thanks to its highly commercialized media system and the cultural valorization of entrepreneurs generally. But this model of entrepreneurial journalism does not play equally everywhere. France, for instance, has a cultural aversion to it.[72] In the Republic of the Congo, developing relationships and pursuing opportunities lead to "brown envelope journalism," meaning bribes are a crucial source of income.[73] In short, the limited opportunities and significant tensions present in personal branding among journalists casts doubt on the effectiveness of entrepreneurialism as a core journalistic value.

Furthermore, value also needs to be assessed in terms of the actual returns—whether professional or financial—journalists and their organizations get for their substantial investment of time and effort into branding. Many news organizations have begun to ask whether social media is "worth it" both financially and in terms of other resources, especially their journalists' time. Some have concluded it isn't and quit.[74] This conversation extends to journalists' branding activities because they (presumably) take time away from other things journalists might be doing and so raise the question of which activities are the most journalistically valuable. While some journalists are concerned with the productive value of branding, others may use branding that is focused more on productive interaction and engagement with users and communities. Similarly, within the frameworks for reciprocity in journalism, acts of personal branding and "caring" can be defined as an exchange between a group of actors that is often mutually beneficial or productive, not just commercially viable.[75] Personal branding practices can also be intimate, affective practices produced by journalists to support online interactions that are both professionally productive and satisfying.

As these complex conversations continue, journalists continue to practice both connection to their audiences and separation from them. They connect their profession to an organization through employment while also testing the waters of personal branding. They struggle to balance personal and professional across multiple platforms while fighting burnout from the emotional labor required to maintain those front-stage performances. While all of this is evidence of hybridity in media logics and practices, it is also paradoxical that something so widely accepted and practiced could also be so troublesome. Journalists and their organizations see value in branding, even if as nothing more than a pragmatic tool. Organizations see branding as a key element of the transparency they hope will resolve crises of trust. They also encourage their employees to get behind efforts to attract and maintain audiences that are increasingly fickle and fragmented. Furthermore, as news organizations have weakened, they have pushed their workers to use branding practices to help shore up the organizational brand and maintain its reputation and image.

What used to be a relatively narrow career ladder with a few prestigious editorial positions at the top is now spread out, with career endpoints that do not always include news organizations or even journalistic work. Translating a devoted following into paying newsletter subscribers is just one option, as illustrated at the start of this chapter. Other options include nonprofit work, foundation work, consulting, lobbying, and a wide range of freelancing and entrepreneurial possibilities. Equally likely is that organizations' push for additional branding work leads news workers toward burnout. Journalists' job descriptions have lengthened as they are asked to assume responsibility for marketing and distributing their own work, not to mention the overall increase in workload due to layoffs and loss of resources. Asking them also to bear responsibility for creating and leveraging a personal persona, alongside some organizational branding work, could lead to burnout. Research has documented that branding work is laden with various kinds of emotional labor in addition to the manual tasks it requires.[76] The feelings of exposure and pressure to be constantly available and engaged on social media are ingredients in a recipe for burnout. Thus, the paradox is that the harder organizations push branding, the less their employees will be able to give to all endeavors and the more likely they may be to find ways to separate themselves from audiences or, at the other end of the spectrum, to go all in and invest in their own solo ventures. In chapter 4 we focus much more on the organizational push to social media use for journalism, especially through use of policy. While journalists have focused their attention on individual personal branding, organizational intervention through social media policy influences the ways journalists connect and disconnect online.

CHAPTER 4

Dis/connecting from Policy and Practice

In 2020 the *Pittsburgh Post-Gazette* suspended journalist Alexis Johnson from covering the Black Lives Matter protests over a tweet that the newspaper claimed showed evidence of "bias": "Horrifying scenes and aftermath from selfish LOOTERS who don't care about this city!!!!!. . . . Oh wait, sorry. No, these are pictures from a Kenny Chesney [an American country singer-songwriter] concert tailgate. Whoops."[1] In response to Johnson's suspension, the Newspaper Guild of Pittsburgh reposted her original viral tweet along with the hashtag #IStandWithAlexis, which led to national news coverage.[2] In Johnson's view, she was only expressing the facts. "Is it biased because I'm talking about a Black issue? Also, what sides are there to racism? . . . I said to the managers that I don't think that talking about racism is a political issue. They begged to differ."[3] Whatever your opinion of the tweet itself or the *Post-Gazette*'s reaction, Johnson's story is emblematic of the difficulties that newsroom social media policies place upon both reporters and their supervisors.

Organizations have used social media policies, which focus heavily on correctly representing brand identity and opinion, as grounds for firing, suspension, and other disciplinary actions against journalists whose social media activity is deemed inappropriate. The difficulty, of course, is that these policies are highly subjective and unevenly enforced, with women and people of color often bearing the brunt of them. The dynamic is so crystallized that instead of individually challenging the *New York Times* for its op-ed calling on the president to use force against civilians, Black *New York Times* employees and their allies responded as a collective on Twitter, all tweeting: "This puts Black *New York Times* staff in danger."[4]

This trend of working in fear of violating company social media policy—sometimes without even knowing precisely what that policy states—is especially difficult for journalists to navigate as they balance semipublic personal and professional identities. This challenge is heightened for journalists historically excluded from the profession, including Black, Hispanic, Latino, and Indigenous journalists. But it's a common concern for many professionals who perform digital media work. Journalists report fearing punishment for transgressing organizational policies, including being barred from covering a topic or even being fired. This fear is based on distressing precedents. In the past few years, it has become increasingly easy to find examples of reporters who have been fired over their social media posts. Australian sports reporter Scott McIntyre was fired by the Special Broadcasting Service (SBS) for a tweet criticizing Australian soldiers posted on Anzac Day, a national holiday commemorating a World War I battle at Gallipoli. *CNN* fired Atlanta-based journalist Octavia Nasr over a tweet praising a late Hezbollah leader. *Washington Post* reporter Wesley Lowrey decided to leave the paper after clashing with editors about his Twitter activity.

Dozens of other examples exist, dealing frequently with controversial subjects that are prominent in the news: racism, police brutality, and gender inequality. On one side are news organizations intent on preserving what little trust they still command among audiences, advertisers, and newsmakers. On the other side are journalists embracing digital tools that afford not just expression but also the potential to build real, civically minded audience engagement and influence. In the middle, attempting to manage the tensions in this relationship, is newsroom social media policy.

The aim of this chapter is to examine the ways newsroom social media policy contributes to the paradoxes of connection that define journalists' social media work. This is accomplished through a review of existing scholarly literature on newsroom social media policy, complemented by discourse analysis of publicly available newsroom policies and industry press about social media work. The literature reviewed covers roughly the last decade, having picked up once newsroom social media use became widespread and even required. The researchers cited in this chapter have studied early newsroom social media policies and interviewed both supervisors and journalists about policy and practice. Synthesis of this literature reveals the themes, trends, and overall development of newsroom social media policy discussed in this chapter.

Because newsroom social media policy is constantly developing and changing, including during the writing of this book, we conducted a discourse analysis of current and publicly available newsroom social media policies.[5] The analysis also included articles about newsroom social media work published in the *Columbia Journalism Review*, the *New York Times*, and other media outlets as cited here. The goal of this discourse analysis was to observe what assumptions underlie the formation and implementation of newsroom social media policy and to observe what values and beliefs are communicated through these policies to the journalists who are expected to follow them.

Together, the discourse analysis and literature review inform an understanding of the paradoxes inherent in newsroom social media policies and explanations for how these policies arise. We find that newsroom social media policies attempt to balance journalists' individual expression online with news organizations' desire to manage employee behavior in a way that minimizes risk to the organization. The result is a set of policies that are often paradoxical in their construction, ineffective in practice, and subjective in enforcement.

These complexities are inflected with various forms of organizational and sociopolitical power, contributing to labor inequalities and precarity for modern news workers. This is important because these policies contribute to and create the paradoxes of connection that define journalists' social media work, adding uncertainty to journalists' already precarious work.

Creating Effective Policy

The purpose of workplace policy generally is to ensure alignment between employee behavior and organizational mission. Workplace policy is a tool of governance and commonly aims to regulate processes and procedures in a business entity.[6] Workplace policies often take an approach of risk management, focusing on safety and seeking to limit liability. In a broader sense, workplace policy is an embodiment of corporate or public values that should guide managerial decision-making and employee work experiences.[7]

As computers and internet access became staples in the workplace, companies of all kinds began seeking ways to encourage proper use of these tools and to limit their misuse. Companies developed internet usage policies governing, for instance, email and personal computer use. Later, companies updated these policies to include and focus on social media use, such that social media policies have become prevalent across all kinds of businesses.[8] For any policy to be effective, scholars have argued that it should be consistent, appropriately limited in scope, and enforceable without bias. There should be a range of enforcement options available (beyond immediate dismissal), and disciplinary decisions should be correctable through appeal.[9] Finally, employees must be involved in creating a policy to aid in adoption and compliance, while managers should be responsible for effectively communicating and enforcing it.[10] But as studies suggest, there is substantial variation in managerial decision-making when responding to disciplinary cases.[11]

Newsrooms have been slower than other organizations to learn these scholarly lessons and craft workplace social media policies accordingly. In 2012 interviews with a range of Flemish journalists found that social media guidelines were scarce.[12] Within a few years, however, most Western news organizations had social media guidelines, if not fully developed policies.[13] Latin American newsrooms appear to be further behind in this process, with one recent survey finding that only about half of journalists worked in a newsroom with a social media policy.[14] Flemish research suggests that journalists are not commonly involved in setting these policies and sometimes don't even know what they are exactly.[15] Research with Australian journalists showed that most policies were assumed to just be "commonsense" extensions of norms of journalistic practice.[16] An exception is the *New York Times'* social media policy, which states that it was shaped by employee input and has been shared publicly.[17]

Early on, newsroom social media policies varied widely, suggesting there was not a common set of concerns or interests shaping them—perhaps with good reason, given the variation in size, audience, and mission among news organizations.[18] Individual newsrooms generally created these policies for themselves, except where authoritarian governments imposed regulations of their own on media.[19] But over the years, some level of consensus has formed around the unique opportunities and risks social media present.[20]

Journalists have noticed a shift in newsroom social media policy away from an emphasis on experimentation and transparency and toward stricter control and reputation management.[21] Journalists have resisted this shift and the explicit policies that attended it. Sociologists have long understood the creation of journalistic norms and processes as a function of social control, but that means of ensuring conformity is being supplanted by explicit policies, at least in the case of social media.[22]

Newsroom social media policies generally seek to maintain a level of "compliance with employer goals and standards."[23] Though there remains substantial variation in these policies, several key themes emerge. Drawing from a close reading of publicly available newsroom social media policies, dominant themes of governance include identity and reputation management, opinion, audience interactions and tone, and privacy.

First, identity and reputation management emerge as the governing principle that determines overall newsroom social media policy. Management of organizations is often based on avoiding the seemingly uncontrollable individualism promoted by social media use; the prioritization of relatability, real talk, opinion, and interactivity are all considered a reputational risk. Newsroom social media policies thus express a clear interest in preserving the image and reputation of the organization by ensuring that corporate identity commands precedence over personal identity for all employees. Consider the following statements from newsroom social media policies:

- "Washington Post journalists are always Washington Post journalists."
- "You must identify yourself as an LAT [*Los Angeles Times*] employee online. . . . Don't write or post anything that would embarrass the LAT."
- "Employees must identify themselves as being from AP if they are using their accounts for work in any way."
- "In social media posts, our journalists must not . . . do anything that undercuts The [New York] Times's journalistic reputation."
- "Journalists participating in social networks need to be aware of the need to protect the agency's image and principles."
- "And always remember, you represent NPR."

In short, newsroom employees must always represent their employer on social media, precluding the possibility of having a personally branded presence online. Even if reporters are using their own personal accounts—that is, accounts not owned by the organization or explicitly labeled as organizational property—policies treat these personal accounts as strongly associated with the organization. "My Twitter account is a Times account," a *New York Times* reporter writes.[24]

Policies can discourage the use of separate personal and professional accounts with the reasoning that both will be associated with the parent organization. Even if outright ownership is not established and is, in fact, difficult to assert legally, journalists are warned that everything they do online is subject to workplace policies.[25] This loss of an online personal identity distinct from one's employer is described as the "price of employment by a major media institution." Yet as chapter 6, on harassment, describes in more detail, the consequences of online connection are nonetheless positioned by organizations as an individual responsibility.[26]

Rather than setting limits on organizational reach such that personal and professional can be separated, these policies reflect a total collapse of both and the hierarchical supremacy of organizational identity.[27] These policies arise because of the ways newsroom managers fear that opinions, interactions, and so on could harm the organizational reputation, and so they seek to manage those risks through policy.

A second theme in social media policy focuses on opinions. Many social media policies suggest that the primary way journalists might damage organizational reputation is by expressing an opinion or doing anything that might be construed as such. The language covering this point is all-inclusive. For example:

- *Washington Post* journalists may not post anything that "could objectively be perceived as reflecting political, racial, sexist, religious, or other bias or favoritism."
- *New York Times* journalists "must not express partisan opinions, promote political views, endorse candidates, make offensive comments or do anything else that appears to take sides."
- "AP [Associated Press] staffers must be aware that opinions they express may damage the AP's reputation as an unbiased source of news."

Newsroom social media policies generally go on to explain that the reason for these limits on opinions is that the organization's primary value proposition is as a trusted and impartial provider of information. Anything that could undercut audience perceptions of that value does direct harm to the organization's bottom line. The policies are not entirely wrong about this—a controlled experiment found that journalists' social media accounts that engaged in more personal disclosure and audience interaction were judged by audience members to be less objective.[28]

Even so, these more personal and interactive accounts boosted intent to read news from the journalist's employer, suggesting that even if objectivity was damaged, the organization benefited overall. The study concluded that audience members value objectivity (or at least the perception of it) less than other factors in determining where to get their news. If so, this position stands in clear contrast to the heavy emphasis on impartiality and objectivity evident in newsroom social media policies.

A third theme addresses online interactions and tone. Newsroom social media policies encourage respectful, considerate dialogue when interacting with others on social media. Policies state that this engagement helps to embed the news organization in the community by making connections with individual people. At the same time, policies seek to limit interactions that may reflect poorly on the journalist and the organization. Journalists are discouraged, for instance, from responding to criticism and complaints. Such interactions, the policies assert, are likely to inflate the problem rather than resolve it. Journalists are also discouraged from offering their own criticism—of their employer, of other journalists, and even of other companies—because, the policies state, any such remarks could be interpreted as representing the news organization's views and either directly or indirectly damage the organization's reputation.[29] Newsroom social media policies suggest discretion regarding which links are shared, which accounts are followed, which groups are joined, and even when to use humor.

Newsroom social media policies contain a smattering of other advice on interactions and tone. Some policies specify that journalists should have and use social media accounts, and all policies encourage positive interactions on social media. Journalists should use social media to showcase their work and that of their colleagues. Openness and honesty are also recurring values in guiding how journalists should approach social media interactions. Policies also encourage transparency in dealing with corrections.

Few of the policies address harassment beyond requesting that the journalist report the offending post to the platform and seek guidance from supervisors. Perhaps further policies exist and are not shared publicly, but recent interviews suggest that support for harassment victims is severely lacking in newsrooms.[30] Beyond this, journalists are warned not to engage with trolls or other bad-faith actors online and to use the platform's affordances to block or mute the offending account.

As a whole, these guidelines on interactions and tone reflect broader organizational and governmental definitions of "digital citizenship" as promoting rational, civil, and profitable social media use and to uphold journalism's role in digital participation as benefiting society as a whole.[31] Of course, this does not reflect the reality of most users' experience of online communication environments as pluralistic and provocative.[32] For journalists, these interactions can also be productive in challenging otherwise fixed social discourses, such as Alexis Johnson's satirical takedown of everyday racism in the United States as part of her Black Lives Matter (BLM) reportage. Yet these productive public interactions can sometimes run counter to organizational policy.

A final theme in social media policy for journalists prioritizes questions of privacy. Newsroom social media guidelines advise journalists that they should have no expectations of privacy online. They are expected to act as if everything they do on social media is part of the public record, no matter what settings or exclusions social media platforms may allow them to impose. Many policies encourage journalists to make use of platform privacy settings to limit the reach of individual posts on social media while also reminding them that even these confidential posts may be copied and reposted elsewhere out of context for wider viewing. Policies specify that individual journalists and not organizations are legally responsible for the things they say on social media. Policies also usually remind journalists that they are subject to the privacy and sharing policies of the platforms themselves, including any terms of conduct the platforms may impose.

Some everyday issues that journalists face online are unevenly addressed across social media policies. Many are inconsistent in their attention to processes of verification. Some make no mention of these processes as relating directly to social media. Others specify that journalists should prioritize face-to-face or phone interactions as a means of gathering new information and verifying information contained in social media posts. The policies reflect a consensus that simply republishing a post in a news story is bad practice. A similar logic is behind cautions against retweeting, or republishing another user's tweet. The guidelines suggest quoting the tweet so that the journalist can add additional context or disclaimers or not retweeting at all if the information in the tweet can't be immediately verified.

These inconsistencies show that professional norms are not fixed across news organizations; therefore, journalists often rely on traditional practices that may not suit social media environments, or they experiment with new practices that may seem innovative but also leave journalists open to breaching organizational policy. Closer attention to these policies also shows that while journalists are increasingly being asked to work online and that their professional branding labor is leveraged to benefit news organizations, journalists are nonetheless being left to deal with any impacts of living and working in complex communication settings. As a whole, these questions of privacy highlight why journalists use disconnection strategies as a way of strategically managing connection with audiences.

Connect, but Remain Disconnected

Newsroom social media policies draw from two sets of logics: editorial logic, or the principles that have traditionally driven news media and their systems, and social media or audience logic, or those norms, standards, and processes that are native to social media platforms and the culture of their users.[33] Because both editorial logic and social media logic are at work in a hybrid media system and because these logics are sometimes in conflict with one another, newsroom social media policies are paradoxical.[34] Newsroom social media policies ask journalists to shoulder the contradictions between social media and editorial logics and attempt to give them guidance in doing so. But they end up presenting a series of paradoxes that journalists have said they struggle to resolve.

The first paradox of social media policy asks journalists to connect but remain disconnected. The theme of disconnection as a means of managing connection on social media is more fully explained in the introduction to this book, but it is recognizable as the principal paradox inherent in newsroom social media policies. At their heart, these policies ask journalists to engage with their sources and their audiences on social media while at the same time maintaining a professional distance from them. This balancing act has long been a part of journalists' close-but-not-too-close relationships with sources. Social media's cultural affordances invite the audience to engage with journalists as well.

As such, social media policies have much more to say about journalists' interactions with their audiences than with their sources over social media. Journalists are encouraged to use social media to build relationships with the audience but are also told to make liberal use of blocking and muting tools to manage disconnections from that audience. Journalists are counseled to seek feedback from audiences and incorporate this feedback into their work but not to respond to criticism on social media for fear of fanning the flames.

The paradox also extends to source interactions, as journalists are allowed to follow sources and potential sources on social media as a means of gathering information. Yet they are cautioned to do this in a balanced way to avoid the appearance of taking sides. The request to exercise good judgment and moderation is reasonable when taken at face value, but in fact it asks journalists to take responsibility for preventing a misperception of bias that audience members may already hold, regardless of a journalist's social media behavior.

The reality is that there is no configuration of a journalist's social network that is unimpeachable or perfectly balanced. Striving for this ideal may be admirable, but the effect of the paradox of connection is that it creates additional labor devoted to managing these connections and disconnections at the risk of suppressing or supplanting other journalistic tasks. It also signals to journalists that maintaining a veneer of objectivity is of greater or at least equal importance than seeking truth and reporting it.

Be Yourself, but Actually Be Us

Social media sites are so named because their primary affordance is establishing connections among people—individuals who express themselves and communicate with each other. Studies of social media have suggested that users imagine an audience when posting, using their perceptions of who might be listening to craft their message.[35] Scholars have also concluded that one of the primary drivers of social media activity is emotion both in posting and in consuming social media.[36] For these reasons, social media sites are inherently personal and relational, as opposed to institutional and instrumental. It's no surprise that best practices on social media revolve around intimate and personalized relationships, and this emphasis is reflected in newsroom social media policies. In other words, to be successful on social media, journalists must be themselves. They must be real and authentic.

Despite this emphasis, it is abundantly clear in newsroom policies that news organizations wish to retain control over their employees' social media activity, reaping for themselves any benefits that may be derived from it. Employees are required to identify themselves as belonging to the news organization. Even their personal social media accounts are considered company property. They must always consider themselves not as individuals but as organizational representatives.

Personal disclosure is risky in terms of perceptions of bias, potential for harassment, and, of course, problematic popularity. One thing news organizations are especially wary of is journalists' potential to use social media—and journalists' affiliation with the news organization—to build a large enough following to strike out on their own, taking value away from the company. As a result, social media policies consistently and clearly convey that a company's journalists and social media work belong to the organization.

This stance is not unexpected, given the way news organizations fear a reorganization of power, shifting attention away from the organization and onto a few of its most prominent journalists. But the policy is paradoxical because it asks journalists to use social media without embracing any of the practices that make it useful and effective in the first place. The policies seem to allow room for little more than staid promotion of the news organization's products, which may be a low-risk strategy but also takes little advantage of social media's affordances. Journalists cannot be both themselves and company shills on social media, and so they are caught between pleasing company supervisors and engaging effectively with audiences. The result is exasperation with policy and a sense that they have lost both autonomy and identity.[37]

Attract Attention, but Not the Wrong Kind

One of the main benefits news organizations see in social media is the potential to attract audiences. This is not about revenue directly, and in fact news organizations make little to no money via social media platforms directly.[38] The reasoning is that social media sites act as an alert system for news, keeping it a prominent (if ambient) part of people's lives, such that audiences are more aware of the news organization and its offerings.[39] Social media also functions as a discovery system for news, allowing users to encounter it incidentally.[40] Thus, newsroom social media policies place considerable emphasis on individual journalists' ability to attract attention to the news organization and its products through responsible use of social media. The policies present this as an opportunity for journalists to be part of the outreach apparatus that increases the visibility of their work.

A paradox arises when policies go on to specify all the ways journalists should avoid attracting attention—by blending in on social media, by acting as a guest, by being an observer, by working as a stagehand rather than as the star performer.[41] Journalists are asked to share the news on social media but are cautioned against becoming the news themselves. Visibility is key in this paradox; news organizations seek greater visibility for the organization and its content while at the same time limiting the accumulation of attention by individual popular journalists. But the mechanism for achieving this is for all individual journalists at the organization to collectively increase their visibility on social media platforms.

Don't Cross the Line, but Where's the Line?

Each of the three preceding paradoxes presents a unique contradiction in the guidance journalists are given within newsroom social media policies. A common element of these paradoxes is that newsroom social media policy often suggests that journalists should remain within the boundaries of acceptable social media use. These policies all constitute efforts to define those boundaries, but rather than create them explicitly, these policies often resort to requesting journalists to exercise good judgment, caution, or wisdom. The policies do not specify whether they may be applied retroactively, imposing consequences for previous indiscretions, though this is a common occurrence for public figures.

The boundaries are therefore both subjective and transient, as well as subject to sudden shifts in popular opinion or culture. Many policies use the analogy that journalists should not do anything on social media they would not do in a published news story while in the same document encouraging them to experiment and try new things.[42] Newsroom social media policies want journalists simultaneously to take no risks and to risk new ventures, provided they are willing to bear any negative consequences themselves.

The paradoxes inherent in newsroom social media policies leave both journalists and the organizations they work for hamstrung. The reasons for these failures lie in the policies' goals, scope, and potential ramifications. A major flaw in newsroom social media policies is that they set such an expansive scope that journalists cannot abide by them and managers cannot enforce them. First, policies convey greater concern with using social media to prevent declines in trust than in using social media to build trust. This is a defensive stance that is perhaps unsurprising, given the global assault against journalism as "fake news" over the past several years. This position assumes, however, that proper use of social media can in fact influence trust in journalism in substantial ways, when in fact both industry observers and scholars find this proposition doubtful.[43] It's difficult to say what, exactly, might help rebuild trust in journalism, which means that asking a social media policy to rebuild that trust is a formula to ensure the policy's failure.[44] Second, it is impossible for policies to account for all possible infractions and to cover all journalists' personal and professional interactions over time. The policies as written leave open the possibility that anything about the journalist's character or actions could be grounds for dismissal if it tarnishes the organizational brand. Even if the scope is limited to decisions a journalist made while employed, tweets don't always age well. Since newsroom social media policies set such an expansive scope (with words like "always"), they are likely to make both adherence and enforcement difficult or even impossible.

Newsroom social media policies undermine themselves by relying almost exclusively on the good judgment of both journalists and their managers. Good policy provides for flexibility in consequences but aims for consistency in definitions and enforcement.[45] It is worth noting that there are positive examples of proactive approaches to policy. After George Floyd was killed by police in Minneapolis in 2020, Kyndell Harkness, managing assistant editor of diversity and community at the *Minneapolis Star Tribune*, said, "There were a number of us in the newsroom who were thinking about what that really meant for us, doing some soul searching in terms of how our paper needed help with equity, and what needs to be said and done."[46] Since then, the newspaper has made efforts to re-create Harkness's role by rewriting newsroom policies, doing internal audits, and fostering spaces for listening, learning, and being open among reporters, among other things, in order to address diversity and equity issues such as employee retention.

This example shows how social media policies can balance the needs of an organization to present reportage that accurately and fairly reflects the public interest, but it also acknowledges the complexity of maintaining this public role in social media environments. Newsroom policies must strike a balance between the social media logics that might foster public trust in these environments and supporting the journalists who take on the risk of creating new practices and interactions that maintain that trust.

This chapter has argued that even though there are differences in how news organizations approach social media policies, a few key themes emerge. Newsroom social media policies are driven by a desire for identity and reputation management. The means to achieve this are a blanket prohibition on opinion, limits on interactivity and tone, and the removal of online privacy expectations. Inherent in these newsroom social media policies are several paradoxes as connection and disconnection, engagement, and distance come into conflict. These paradoxes arise from newsrooms' need to balance opportunity and risk and from newsrooms seeking to balance editorial and social media (or audience) logics in a hybrid media system.

This balancing act results in paradoxical policies that instruct journalists to engage with their audiences while also representing the company and sharing very little of themselves and none of their opinions. Practically, the policies are ineffective despite newsrooms' best efforts because they are too broad in scope and too subjective in nature. Meanwhile, journalists who don't want their next tweet to be their last must steer well clear of gray areas and controversial subjects. This is a far cry from how journalism has often been portrayed: as a watchdog, an agitator or adversary, an institution meant to hold those in power to account.

PART III

Connection and Disconnection for Changing Journalistic Practice

CHAPTER 5

Connecting with Journalism in an Era of Misinformation

Amid the initial global outbreak of the COVID-19 virus in 2020, the Australian government response to the pandemic was lauded for successfully using border closures and state-based lockdown measures to keep infection and death at some of the lowest rates in the world. By early 2021, and with a growing Delta-variant outbreak, Australia's national vaccination rates were languishing at almost last of all of the Organization for Economic Co-operation and Development (OECD) nations.[1] Vaccine hesitancy was also very strong among people aged fifty to sixty, those most likely to be hospitalized by the virus. Health statistics indicate that the very specific demographics of Australians exhibiting vaccine hesitancy was the result of missed opportunities by governments and health officials to counter misinformation and disinformation about the pandemic on social media.[2] Public health experts and governments have struggled with the public's thirst for information about the pandemic, especially the difficulty of translating complicated information about the source of the virus, its effects, and potential solutions.

For journalists around the world, the pandemic's informational challenges have been manyfold. Among others, first, journalists have been challenged to report on often complicated epidemiological information accurately and effectively. Second, journalists have had to mediate increasing public scrutiny of health information resulting from dedicated misinformation and disinformation campaigns. Finally, alternate and often aggressively anti-mainstream media players have been competing with professional journalism for attention and credibility. Professional journalists have been caught up in the effects of public mistrust of large-scale public institutions, governance, and media organizations, especially with media players and campaigns that have purposely used antivaccination sentiment to discredit them. Further, journalists may not be the central authority on news and information in social media spaces, as audiences are increasingly exposed to influencer-driven information when looking for news.

As we have argued in the introduction to this book, the heart of the issue for journalists is the paradox of connection. The same media tools that have made it much easier for journalists to connect with audiences also increasingly fuel disconnection between journalists and audiences competing to have the loudest and most influential voice, especially in social media spaces. In chapter 4 we explored the organizational policy frameworks aimed at formalizing the norms of online connection available to journalists on social media. In this chapter we extend our focus to the ways social media logics complicate these traditional forms of journalistic connection online, particularly in environments where traditional norms of reportage are presented as obstructing audience agency in accessing information. To do so, we explore some of the impacts that poor reporting practices had on the public during the pandemic and what other journalists have been doing to regain public trust online.

Misinformation and Disinformation in Online News Flows

Disinformation refers to false or misleading information intentionally spread to create harm or to advance political goals, as opposed to misinformation, which refers to false information spread unintentionally.[3] Research suggests that disinformation narratives build on and reify preexisting ideologies, such as those involving race and inequality. Identity-based hierarchies, like politics about gender and race, often play a key role in the creation, spread, and uptake of disinformation narratives. Misinformation, on the other hand, has been seen to spread due to political agreement and emotional reaction to news and information, especially in friendship and family groups.

The global pandemic has highlighted the connections between increasing digital propaganda in online information flows and its bearing on individual and group political identity. Journalists have been overwhelmed by the aggressive dismissal of mainstream journalism as "fake news" and the number of voices in the public sphere vying for authority over information flows. The speed and intensity of the change have been exacerbated by the pandemic, especially at its beginnings, because the public's thirst for information has been matched by the number and vigor of challenges to what would once have been considered unassailable facts.

The first challenge journalists face is that, increasingly, audiences report that they do not trust the mainstream media. This is contextualized within a broader mistrust of public institutions in Western nations, aligned with a sense that contemporary institutions and the methods of accountability associated with them are fundamentally broken.[4] While trust in the media has been declining steadily in the United States since the 1970s, survey research showed that attention to news grew during the pandemic by almost 25 percent. However, the survey suggested that about half of US adults got much of their vaccine news on social media.[5] In Australia, trust in the media grew during 2020 due to public interest in news about the pandemic but receded the next year to the global average of 43 percent.[6] Further research has shown that Australian news consumers based trust of news on the particular outlet they habitually used much more than on individual journalistic practices.[7] These results point to decreasing audience perception of the relevance of professional journalism to their everyday lives. Other research showed audiences saw news consumption as a by-product rather than a goal of their daily online use and preferred an algorithm selecting news for them based on previous use rather than a journalist or news editor.[8]

Second, audiences increasingly suggest that their own research and news habits do a far better job of informing them than a journalist might. Several research studies have shown that consumers are overconfident about their ability to assess whether social media content contains misinformation. One study showed that while participants from across the political spectrum were in agreement that misinformation should be labeled for others, they were equally confident they could identify misinformation without labels.[9] Another study by Jacob Nelson and Seth C. Lewis showed that respondents felt capable of corroborating information presented on mainstream news with their own research.[10] Participants suggested that repetition of information from different sources made them more inclined to believe it was true, reinforcing Jay Van Bavel and colleagues' argument that user exposure to disinformation promotes its veracity, which in turn furthers its spread.[11] Further work by Anna Staender and colleagues showed that while disinformation was often presented in an emotional or sensationalist style, the average user was more likely to agree with disinformation if it was presented in a neutral way.[12] Users are also more likely to share disinformation because they want to demonstrate support for the point of view it espouses, thus suggesting the importance of political and social identification in the distribution of misinformation.[13]

The political focus on social media identity has also intersected with the online cultures that celebrate the influence of individuals in political and cultural groups. Further, the commercialized nature of social media information environments and their associated attention economies has also meant that audiences using social media are identifying with personas that reflect social and political information using an attention-grabbing, emotional, and sometimes even polarizing style (see also chapter 1).[14] These personas tend to encourage affective responses to their content and center their own personality and experiences to news and information, which can provide opportunities for the spread of misinformation.[15] Studies in India and Chile found that social media messaging services strongly contribute to political news exposure.[16] The intimate nature of these platforms and social identification between users influence trust of the information shared. Users encountering news through social media, whether engaging with commercial influencers or connecting with friends and family in more intimate social media spaces, appear to increasingly place trust in the social and political identity of the sharer. This further distances professional journalism from the role of producing or moderating news and information.[17]

All these factors—distrust, disillusionment, and disinformation—point to larger issues within journalism's connection to audiences. Social media environments privilege individual modes of expression, reflected in both the growing reliance on individual professional self-promotion online and the status given to individuals fostering online personas based on perceptions of authenticity and intimate connection. Traditionally, this connection was based on journalists' privileged role as a public service and audiences' dependence on the daily news as one of the only ways to be reliably informed. This role provides not only a social framework for connection with audiences but also a kind of security that journalists' practices are conducive to appropriate professional behavior.[18]

Social media has created new opportunities for journalists to bring news practices to new audiences. It has also created challenges in an increasingly crowded informational sphere, where journalists compete with new media players who work solely on new media platforms and do not have to adapt existing methodologies and professional ideologies to the unique logics and cultures of social media platforms. Journalists and news organizations also compete for the attention of audiences who believe that much of the news and information created by professional journalists is biased. These same audiences are guided by algorithms that prioritize their personal preferences and often erroneously believe they know which sources to trust. Susceptibility to misinformation during the global pandemic was never seen as a personal issue, and thus misinformation spread like a virus that "no one thinks they can get . . . only everyone else."[19] These tensions were made more obvious during the COVID-19 pandemic, when journalists have faced labor pressures due to decreasing numbers in the industry, the speed with which information is required, and the number of dissenting voices in media environments.

COVID-19 Rollout: Eroding and Establishing Trust in Journalism

In late 2020 the Australian government confirmed that it had sourced Pfizer and AstraZeneca for the COVID-vaccine rollout to commence the next year.[20] The AstraZeneca vaccine would be administered to individuals age sixty and above, while the Pfizer vaccine, bought in lesser quantities in the first stage of the rollout, would be recommended for younger people. The staged vaccination was flawed from the beginning. While most of Australia had staved off mass illness and hospitalization through strict lockdown measures, this work was squandered by not rolling out vaccinations while the virus had been all but eradicated. When the first vaccines finally arrived in Australia in February 2021, the prime minister had promised that the vaccine would be offered to every Australian adult by October, suggesting that the rollout was "not a race."[21] But a lack of logistical focus on mass vaccination and a failure to secure a consistent vaccine supply meant increasingly aggressive news reportage about the slow, cumbersome, and unnecessarily complex system of vaccination.[22]

Increased critical reporting on the rollout also increased journalistic focus on the vaccine itself. Journalists began reporting a very rare side effect of the AstraZeneca vaccine: increased risk of thrombosis with thrombocytopenia, or potentially fatal blood clots, for those under sixty years old. While there is a small risk of thrombosis in those age sixty and over, it is lower than in younger people.[23] Each time someone suffered a side effect, even a relatively minor side effect, it was reported and often headlined the news. Despite the relative lack of risk to those over fifty, Victoria's most-read newspaper, the *Herald Sun*, reported that AstraZeneca was being dropped as the government's preferred vaccine for over fifties with the headline "Flirting with DisAstra?"[24]

Australia's public service broadcaster, the ABC, also reported that a woman's death was reported to the Therapeutic Goods Administration as a precautionary measure, though there was no evidence she died from a blood clot, and she had received a vaccination more than a month prior to her death.[25] A story that otherwise would never have been considered newsworthy was nonetheless

published by the national broadcaster in a flurry of media attention on a compa-
rably minuscule risk. Doctors began publicly warning that over fifties had begun
canceling their vaccination appointments after reading about the potential for
blood clotting, despite being at lower risk.[26]

The material impacts of poor governmental communication and sensationalist reporting remain: Australians age fifty to sixty remain the least vaccinated
demographic in Australia and the most likely to indicate vaccine hesitation. This
is just one example that shows how politicized and sensationalist reportage can
have a social impact. It leads to the kind of reportage that audiences in Western
liberal democracies are taught through media literacy education to distrust. It
also adds weight to claims from growing numbers of people who suggest that
doing their own research might avoid sensationalized information.[27] Further,
sensationalist reporting about AstraZeneca side effects created space for alternative media stakeholders to fill the void of trust for governmental advice
with something quite different: an antivaccination sentiment.

Social Media Influence and Finding Journalistic Connection

Antivaccination misinformation and disinformation related to COVID-19 on
social media appear to be a comparatively small but potentially harmful phenomenon, linked with existing online behaviors that contribute to declines in
childhood immunization rates. Social media behaviors such as posting individual vaccine injury stories, dismissing vaccination efficacy to prefer individual
immunity, and forwarding political conspiracy have been widely established
within antivaccination online groups and co-opted into the emerging COVID-19
antivaccination discourse.[28] At the beginning of the Australian vaccine rollout,
a small but determined group of antimask and antivaccination campaigners
made a political impact in Australia largely online but also spilling out into
occasional "freedom" rallies. Posting mainly on social media and on private
messenger services, this group presented mainstream media reportage as com-
plicit in lying about the pandemic and vaccine and created alternative media
content to back their claims.

Among this group of antivaccination information providers, three influencers became prominent in Australian online communities by leveraging their
antivaccination views to brand their profiles: Anna Rose (@annarose_co), a
self-described "self-love" guru aligned with Far Right and anti-immigration
politicians; former mom-blogger Leila Stead (@theleilarae); and Taylor Win-
terstein (@tays_way_), a Fijian QAnon-aligned wellness blogger claiming
to speak on behalf of indigenous people.[29] Each used techniques to normalize

antivaccination sentiment. These included setting up new profiles dedicated to antivaccination content, using Instagram Stories and other ephemeral social media to spread misinformation quickly, and creating a protest aesthetic where influencers were photographed in fashionable clothing in posed and filtered selfies from rallies.

By leveraging antivaccination sentiment to boost their personal branding and online businesses, each influencer drew both large followings and intense criticism. Much of the relational labor these influencers practiced was based on creating an in-group of wellness-aligned community members who were spoken to as if they were friends. Many of their claims forwarded their own fearlessness at speaking against the mainstream media acceptance of vaccination, suggesting to their followers that they took on the burden of external criticism to fight for their followers' freedom from apparent oppression. These influencers also attempted to legitimize their stance by using health-based misinformation and messages from sources claiming to be healthcare workers. Every time Twitter or YouTube blocked one of these videos, people commenting on it took it as proof that its misinformation was therefore true.[30] Influencers aligned this emotional information about health and well-being with the social and political identities of users/followers.

The posts espousing misinformation were positioned as a sign of their followers' bravery, uniqueness, and awareness, a way to bring their community together. The virologist David Bauer, whose own words were misappropriated by antivaccination influencers as "proving" the low efficacy of vaccines, suggested: "Part of the appeal of such misinformation is that it restores a sense of agency to people who lack a sense of control over their own lives. It makes people feel part of a 'tribe' of those in the know."[31] While Australian journalists are bound by law, organizational policy, and professional ethics to maintain connection with audiences based on reportage of factual events, these social media influencers were able to leverage personal and intimate connections to unify their followers around their own vaccination message.

The "antivax" discourses raised the ire of provaccination influencers, especially those aligned with feminist activism who began using their profiles to "name-and-shame" prominent antivaccination influencers. Writer and influencer Clementine Ford (@clementine_ford) and actor and influencer Sarah Bartolo (@sarahtbartolo) were vocal in their opposition to antivaccination sentiment in online wellness communities. They expressed their opposition by repurposing traditionally feminist slogans such as "my body, my choice" and by describing the negative impact vaccine hesitancy would have on vulnerable Australian indigenous communities.

Bartolo took a regulation approach to antivaccination sentiment online, starting a Change.org petition to Instagram to deplatform the three antivaccination influencers. While Stead successfully took legal action to have her name removed from the petition, it still garnered almost ten thousand signatures. She also created online skits with characters satirizing antivaccination wellness influencers and encouraging in-group mockery of their stance. Similarly to antivax influencers, Ford created a second account called "Clem loves vaccines," though this solely promoted vaccination science. She also took a "name-and-shame" approach in her stories and posts on her first account, posting screenshots of antivaccination messages with text overlays explaining why a particular message was misinformation, or mocking the poster.

The result of these various influencers' actions was an increasingly aggressive online back-and-forth between influencers, who used Instagram stories to post "gotcha moments" to discredit, shame, and mock each other. The audience effect was that each group of influencers would encourage online group identification according to how they reacted to the others' posts, with users encouraged to report, comment, and share information. Both groups of influencers found themselves at different times being banned from different Instagram affordances like direct messaging, removed from news feeds, and shadow banned.

This in-fighting between different online communities over the veracity of information and popularity is a good example of how difficult it is for journalists to engage with audiences in social media environments, especially within their personalized and commercialized logics of attention. As Crystal Abidin suggests, social media influence is its own systematic and professionalized form of media career. Influence is based on expert use of platform-specific environments to formalize personas for reputation, attention, and, subsequently, commercial benefit.[32] Even "influencer wars," the short, intense, and, importantly, purposeful fueling of discord between online users, allow influencers to gain attention.[33] Even forms of negative attention allow influencers to better present their claims to authenticity and bolster their online tribes of followers, who are invited to display and participate in their affiliation to a particular influencer.

Influencers often have much larger followings than individual journalists and use communication techniques that would not be acceptable as professional journalism. While attention and commercialization may be at the heart of a media organization's priorities, they are not the currency used to draw audiences around individual journalists. Journalists have instead had to find other ways to negotiate social media logics around attention and the public service ideals central to journalism.

Adapting Journalism to Social Media Logics

For those working with traditional reporting practices based on a relatively unified social structure and informational need, the multitude of online identities has muddied journalists' influence as truth bearers. This has required rethinking about practices of connection with audiences. While Australian journalists reported broadly on antivaccination sentiment fueling antilockdown protests, they did not engage with the online influencers fueling this sentiment. Some of the techniques used by influencers to gain attention, such as posting controversial opinions about events or government actors, would be impossible for journalists bound by a code of ethics, organizational policy, and legacy media law and regulation.[34]

Changing information environments have meant that journalists using social media have had to adapt existing practices to media spheres with vastly different cultures of use.[35] While some journalists are integrating their journalistic sensibilities into online relational practices, others are engaging in practices in line with visibility and influence cultures. For some journalists, this has meant moving away from traditional journalistic methods of representation and adapting to social and behavioral norms specific to online influence. This has often meant that journalists have had to negotiate different cultures of visual and textual expression, posting, and intimate disclosure within a culture of practices that value both authenticity and attention-getting strategies.[36] In chapter 3 we showed how journalists use online branding practices to gain attention for their work in online spaces, including posting selfies as a professional self-presentation technique, addressing audiences directly in "real-talk" video posts, and mimicking influencers by posting seemingly banal but authentic information from journalists' personal lives.

Other journalists differ in their approach to social media and appear more focused on interaction and engagement with users and communities based on news interest. As discussed in chapter 1, affective or relational labor is the mostly unremunerated and unacknowledged work content creators like journalists do to engage authentically with audiences who have an interest in their content. Research has shown that this type of community building and engagement builds an online persona that is based on authenticity and that can be leveraged to increase engagement with professional work.[37] Other research has shown that labor to create an engaged community of followers was a way to combine labor with both professional values and personal enjoyment.

Apart from disconnecting from platforms that have negative impacts, deep connection with users on a platform they enjoy using has been described by journalists as a way to find solace, pleasure, or satisfaction in a crowded and labor-intensive communication environment.[38] The business model used by these journalists may require authentic or intimate posting to link back to paid work, but the need for authenticity does not always have a direct promotional or commercial link. Journalists may also facilitate these practices to create safe and enjoyable places to work within a community of followers who are interested in what journalists are reporting and who engage with that reportage through the experiences of the journalist.

Journalists incorporating relational practices into reportage mediate traditional and new forms of professional practice, and these are expressed through understanding the platform and its culture. In the context of COVID-19 pandemic reporting, these traditional journalistic values, expressed through social media logics of intimacy and authenticity, have been one way of combating vaccine misinformation.

Sharnelle Vella is the state political reporter in Victoria, Australia, for television broadcast news at Channel 7. Her following and her professional impact grew exponentially on her Twitter account during the pandemic. Indeed, she almost quadrupled her Twitter following in three months by becoming ordained on the platform as the "Queen of Facts." Vella suggested that her decision to create the daily "Who Wants Facts?" thread partly stemmed from her initial disconnection from Twitter during Victoria's first lockdown: "Last year [2020] I had turned my notifications off for Twitter, and it would give me anxiety to even look at the app. People were angry, and they were angry at the media. There was little a journalist could say on Twitter without being attacked or trolled."[39] During that original point of disconnection, Vella attended the daily press conferences where the premier of Victoria, Daniel Andrews, gave pandemic-related updates. She realized after seeing public criticism of the "nasty" question time that much of the public didn't understand the work of journalism: "The public were seeing how we operate, and it didn't make any sense to them. We definitely made mistakes. I think we lost our way a little bit about what the public actually cared about."[40] This realization showed Vella that a much-needed point of connection with Victorian news audiences was missing on social media: "I had more information sitting in my email inbox than what was actually making it into my news stories each night. . . . Basically I thought—I'm going to throw this all online, just the facts, and you can all decide how you feel about the covid situation. I realized the less opinion I offered—the more people enjoyed the content. That's also why the facts seem to work. People didn't want the opinions and fear—they just wanted the facts." The journalist had realized something that antivaccination influencers had been exploiting during the pandemic. By understanding the locked-down Victorian public's need for community identification, she was more likely to connect with online audiences. Vella combined this realization with a journalistic sense of serving the public interest by sorting politicized reportage from the facts of the state's experience of the pandemic; thus, the daily "Who Wants Facts?" thread was born.

Every day after finishing work at Channel 7, Vella distilled COVID-19 infection numbers and vaccination rates across Australia into "Who Wants Facts?" Her daily thread of national pandemic facts became a trusted resource among the cacophony of often-politicized reporting during the pandemic, punctuated with Vella's use of friendly and irreverent language. (She called followers "besties" and occasionally ended the thread with a "fun fact" or even sports results.) Vella said this style of posting was both her negotiation of journalistic expression in the space and her understanding of audience need: "I've always been much more casual on Twitter than I am on the news. I've probably shown more of my personality there. I think we're at the point where we are learning to live with this virus, and we don't want to be scared or spoken down to. Delivering the facts in a casual way makes them easier to read and understand."[41] Though the daily threads have achieved over thirty-nine million reads since Vella began posting them, she admitted that they were enormously labor-intensive. The information she posted was updated throughout the day and triple verified for accuracy before posting at 7:30 p.m. every evening. She received no financial incentive for posting and no organizational support. Her reason for continuing the posts was centered instead on serving the public interest and upholding her own professional ideals: "The reason I keep doing it is because people look forward to them. We may work for organizations, but our role is to inform the public. No one becomes a journalist because it's a 9 to 5 job—and you certainly don't become a journalist to get paid for all the work you do! You're never really off the clock. I feel like they're helping people navigate the noise of the day." The amount of labor involved in curating the tweet threads meant that Vella discontinued posting "the facts" once Australia's vaccination rate reached 80 percent. She decided that point would signal the end of public need for constant pandemic reportage.

Vella's experience shows that navigating the cultural affordances of platforms like Twitter, with its mélange of news, opinion, commentary, and self-promotion, often makes it difficult both to find quality information and to safely share it. She brought her strong belief in the public service ideal of journalism to counter misinformation peddled by antivaccination influencers: "As a journalist I'm bound by a code of ethics however influencers are not. Throughout the pandemic I've seen some influencers post information that's incorrect, that's exaggerated or that's just downright harmful. More recently I've seen this with Victorian influencers posting incorrect information about suicide rates—with no insight into why the media don't openly talk about suicides or why we report them in the way we do."[42] While journalists cannot always compete directly with the commercialized logics of influencer style content, Vella's threads illustrate the value of verifiable and ethical information during the pandemic. In redirecting her use of the platform toward fact-based reportage, she created a relatively safe space to connect authentically with audiences and to protect her own labor. These actions focused on the relational labor of promoting interaction and engagement with online communities as a form of public service.

Vella's tweets were what she perceived as a spontaneous act of giving back to members of the online community who are most interested in her reportage but who are now an important part of her professional connection to her audiences: "I like to think they're a 'safe space' for people on the internet to get the information they need without the stress or anxiety of watching a press conference. Some people have said they find it better for their mental health. It has carved out somewhat of a safe space on the internet which is nice."[43] While influencers draw a community around themselves, journalists sharing a personal passion for news or issues change their use of social media from simply a commercial or promotional tool into a relational engagement with an online community. It is here that the value proposition for journalism can begin to be articulated on social media.

In a global pandemic, the informational stakes are high. The public need for good information about vaccination is high, and underreportage of side effects can stoke the flames of conspiracy. In this context, publishing every report of a side effect can also potentially distort understanding of the minuscule risk of side effects, as the Australian media's reportage of the side effects of the AstraZeneca vaccine showed. Creating proportional reporting and maintaining public trust are key to maintaining the relevance of journalism. Both require strong audience connection; however, during the pandemic and its resulting tide of information, this connection has been increasingly difficult to maintain. Building trust on social media has been most successfully applied by journalists and organizations that express a clear vision and strategy for contributing to the public good online.

Bolstering Trust and Value through Journalistic Connection

There are examples of media organizations working on using deep connections to research and to social issues to bolster the value of their reportage to audiences. The Bhekisisa Centre for Health Journalism in South Africa is an independent media organization that focuses on solutions-based reportage focused on health issues, which is distributed through news organizations across Africa. Bhekisisa began life as an award-winning specialist health desk for the legacy South African news outlet *Mail and Guardian*. After leaving the *Mail and Guardian* with seven journalists, Bhekisisa received funding from the Bill and Melinda Gates Foundation and has now expanded to nine full-time staff members, two consultants, and ten freelance journalists from across Africa. What is clear from Bhekisisa's reportage during the COVID-19 pandemic is that journalists have disconnected from some social media logics such as immediacy and attention but bolstered others such as transparency when they have served the organization's larger strategic goals for the type of journalism produced. In this way, disconnection practices boost strategic connection in ways that serve broader professional ideals.

Founder and editor-in-chief Mia Malan has suggested that Bhekisisa's goal is to influence health policy in South Africa, where the effects of inequity around access to healthcare and medical information are still being felt. To do this, Bhekisisa's journalists are trained to use evidence-based reporting practices, including only using original sources and relying on peer-reviewed journal studies and reliable statistics to support the storytelling in their reportage. The organization invests in intensive training for each of its journalists and partners with community groups to teach evidence-based, solutions journalism to local journalists.[44] Bhekisisa sends journalists out to small communities to get to know local health issues intimately and works with community media in partnership to create narrative journalism that national news media would be more likely to publish. Malan said that journalists build deep connections with local communities and local issues, using scientifically accurate health reportage to "frame health reporting as not just a medical issue but a social justice issue, because in a country like South Africa this is a crucial issue when there's so much inequality and health plays such a crucial role in daily lives."[45]

Malan suggested that this training builds trust with decision-makers that their reportage is accurate and verifiable. Building this reputation has meant that Bhekisisa's audience has been primarily "policymakers and academics and scientists." During the pandemic the organization found its audience broadening because ordinary citizens needed to understand health information about the pandemic. Much of Bhekisisa's homepage was dedicated to coverage of the COVID-19 pandemic across Africa, with much of the reportage interpreting data and engaging with research, alongside interviews and stories about the personal impact of the pandemic.

Malan suggests that the South African context for the rollout of COVID-19 vaccines has been marred by the lack of good-quality governmental health information in the aftermath of the Zuma administration's depletion of government department budgets and lack of access to vaccines. Across Africa, vaccine hesitancy should be seen in the context of significant vaccine shortages; low vaccination rates have also been caused by problems with the overall vaccine rollout due to structural issues, especially inequity in supply.[46] A 2020 Africa Center for Disease Control (CDC) survey in fifteen countries showed that people with high levels of hesitancy were also more likely to have been exposed to misinformation on social media.[47] In the early stages of the virus, the survey showed that half believed the virus was linked to 5G technology. More recent research shows that vaccine hesitancy is lifting as the impact of the pandemic is felt across Africa. Some conspiracy-linked hesitancy, as well as distrust of governments linked to the vaccine rollout, remains.[48]

At the beginning of the pandemic, Malan made strategic decisions about what Bhekisisa would cover with the very small team. Given that the South African health department has been mired by lack of resourcing, claims of corruption, and deals to roll out Russia's unproven Sputnik vaccine, Malan and her team made two decisions about how to serve their audiences. The first decision would be to use evidence-based reportage to equip policy-makers with good evidence to make science-based decisions about the vaccination rollout. As she suggested, "In a pandemic that is fast moving, you cannot equip people to hold the government accountable if you don't give them the basic science, because if they don't understand the basic science, they wouldn't know what a policy needs to look like. If you don't understand what a vaccine can and can't do, then you wouldn't know how to hold the government accountable to do a good rollout or to not approve certain use of certain vaccines."[49] The second strategic decision was to bolster social media and video reportage to create short health explainers for audiences to understand how and where to get vaccinated, information that Malan said has become de facto governmental public health advice about the pandemic. Bhekisisa also adopted the use of Twitter for shorter, pandemic-related news updates, something the analysis-focused organization had not previously invested in.

Bhekisisa's social media style of reportage was adapted to adhere to its slow, evidence-based style of reportage, with each of its threads taking about two hours to produce. Malan suggests that the organization has also taken time to interact with online audiences and produce reportage inspired by questions the online community has about the pandemic in South Africa. Much like Indigenous X in Australia, this gives voice to otherwise marginalized groups and has created its own community of experts on the platform: "There's a community, and I no longer have to answer all the questions. There are people answering if they ask something; there will be someone who jumps in and answers. It's almost like you create this community that supports each other and that's growing all the time. And that is part of equipping people with the tools to not just lift their daily lives in a safe way but to also understand how to hold a conversation with the evidence." Malan admits that increased social media presence has meant negative pushback from those invested in spreading antivaccination misinformation online. Her background as an HIV reporter working in a country living with the world's largest HIV epidemic had prepared her for this. Bhekisisa ignores antivaccination discourses altogether: "No one knows denialism better than South Africa because of our HIV history. All the research shows you that if you want to address vaccine hesitancy in a country, you should just ignore the small percentage of antivax [*sic*], and you should go for the people who are fence sitters."[50] Malan suggests that reporting on everything that occurs during the pandemic, including governmental spats and the malevolence of antivaccination actors, can result in the politicization of a crisis that requires high-quality, evidence-based analysis to better guide public action. By centralizing its organizational goals of policy change and the value of its skill set in evidence-based reporting, Bhekisisa can better articulate reportage in response to public need rather than simply being reactive to all news.

Bhekisisa's work in evidence-based health journalism is an example of how media organizations can establish their value proposition to audiences by making media tools and their affordances work for an established strategic purpose. It is also an example of just how much time and resourcing is needed to establish trust with diverse audiences in dynamic media spaces. Bhekisisa has institutional support to specialize in evidence-based reporting, to train others, and, most importantly, to take the time to style its interactions with audiences in a way that drives deeper connection and trust over time. For larger mainstream news organizations and their journalists, the need for organizational support to maintain a deep connection to audiences is clear; however, this connection needs to show the value of the journalistic skill set and result in reportage that establishes a connection not just to public interest but also in the service of public need. Only then can the myriad tools of connection be used in a way that molds journalism to the public interest and not simply to the ever-waning attention economies of users.

At a time when journalism's centrality in the provision of news and information seems to be eroding, journalists are encountering a crisis of connection: the struggle to retain trust and relevance with diverse audiences and within different media environments and their competing affordances and logics. The question of how to do this is complicated, but at its heart, journalists and news organizations need to define their value and connection to diverse audiences within diverse and changing media cultures. The consequences of getting the value proposition of good reporting wrong can be seen in Australia's rollout of the AstraZeneca vaccine.

Savvier journalists are incorporating elements of influencer practices to shape how their reportage is received on social media, but there are much more wide-ranging impacts on journalistic practices to connect audiences with news. The examples in this chapter show that journalists must still bring trust, credibility, and meaning to audiences, regardless of the way connection to those audiences changes on different media platforms. As Claudia Mellado and Alfred Hermida suggest, "Trust persists as a key pillar in journalism and remains one of the key ways that journalism distinguishes itself from other forms of public communication. However, trust here lies in the individual journalist, rather in the news publisher they represent."[51] Journalists are now having to connect to online communities using their individual persona, and their work is no longer seen to be solely promoting a media organization. For individual journalists to find a way through this environment requires institutional and organizational support for new forms of connection to audiences not as experts but as trusted community service providers in times of crisis. The role, purposes, and place of journalism within these different media spheres need to be examined, and modes of connection that augment the labor of journalism rather than taking from it need to be designed both through policy and institutional support and by the journalists themselves.

The risks of leaving this labor to individual journalists without the organizational time, support, and mentoring to develop new skills for audience connection on social media leave an increasingly important part of journalistic labor to be squandered and eventually drowned out in an increasingly loud media sphere by those who have more ability to gain attention. Journalists risk having to negotiate agonistic, aggressive, and sometimes abusive interactions on social media alone. In the following chapter, we focus on the ways that fostering deeper connection with audiences on social media can sometimes be harmful to journalists, especially to women and people of color.

CHAPTER 6

Harassment and Disconnection in Journalism's Digital Labor

When former *Fox News* commentator Tucker Carlson decided to attack the *New York Times* technology journalist Taylor Lorenz in March 2021, he didn't just suggest that she was "far younger" and "less talented" than her colleagues. He suggested that she should be grateful for any attention she received for her work, even if, as Lorenz suggested, most of it was online abuse. In a *Fox News* segment discussing "people claiming to be powerless," Carlson said that Lorenz was "at the top of journalism's repulsive food chain" of *New York Times* reporters. He added: "You'd think Taylor Lorenz would be grateful for the remarkable good luck that she's had. But no, she's not." Carlson then read Lorenz's tweet posted for the 2021 International Women's Day, which sought to support women enduring online harassment.[1]

What Carlson didn't mention was that Lorenz had been leading a public call to support female and Black, Indigenous, and People of Color (BIPOC) colleagues facing online harassment, something she had been dealing with personally. Her plea to distinguish "Twitter drama" from online harassment and abuse led to her advocacy for the Online Violence Response Hub, a coalition of global organizations working to find better solutions to online abuse, harassment, and other forms of digital attacks. The hub's work is also supported by two nonprofits, the International Women's Media Foundation (IWMF) and the International Center for Journalists (ICFJ), as well as by professional organizations, academic institutions, journalism-focused nonprofits, and other media organizations.

Carlson's attacks are not new. His efforts at commentary have often resulted in a multitude of attacks from trolls on his targets, most often journalists not aligned with his political views. This trend highlights the rise of mob censorship, a "bottom-up, citizen vigilantism aimed at disciplining journalism" that is "linked to the demonization of journalists and the press by populist leaders."[2] In October 2020 *NBC News* responded to his attack on one of their journalists working to uncover conspiracy theories and online extremism, saying that Carlson "dangerously and dishonestly targeted one of those journalists. Brandy Zadrozny['s] work is widely respected and has contributed greatly to the public's awareness and understanding of the dangers of this alt-universe that breeds online, but has very tangible real-world impacts."[3] For media personalities like Carlson, however, criticizing journalists is fair game. Critique—even fierce critique—should be expected. During these events, Carlson positioned himself not as an attacker but as a watchdog of the press in his role as commentator. It is his repeated assertion that this is a legitimate role for him, for the public invested in news, and even for the journalists that produce it.

Despite Carlson's claims, research shows that online abuse of journalists, especially women, BIPOC, and LGBTQ+ journalists, is impacting on journalists' online labor and creating "anti-journalist rhetoric on social media."[4] Julie Posetti argues: "There are three main converging safety threats confronting women journalists in the digital age: online harassment and abuse against women journalists; orchestrated disinformation campaigns targeting women journalists; and digital privacy and security threats exploiting women journalists' vulnerabilities."[5] A UNESCO-commissioned report drawing on a survey of 901 journalists from 125 countries showed that those with diverse cultural backgrounds faced the worst online harassment. The report also found consistent online violence in the form of physical threats, misogyny mixed with racism, homophobia, religious bigotry, and other forms of discrimination designed to belittle journalists and undermine public trust in their reportage.[6] Female journalists around the world have also said that trolling is constant and in some cases part of concerted campaigns to discredit them; this abuse often mixes threatening commentary to deliberately provoke response with legitimate criticism of their journalism to undermine their complaints.[7] A study by African Women in Media (AWiM) found that more than half of women journalists surveyed experienced increased online harassment during the COVID-19 pandemic.[8] Other research has shown that female journalists feel that online violence has been normalized in their work experience, and many have been forced to change their working practices, even disguising their professional identity, to avoid harm and abuse.[9]

This chapter illustrates how organizations and community organizations have supported journalists to cope with harassment online and offline. Previous chapters in this book have explored the multiple forms of connection and disconnection inherent in journalism's online labor and their impact on new forms of digital labor in journalism. These chapters have focused on the paradoxes inherent in maintaining online connection. Unsurprisingly, as traditional norms of public dialogue online change and often become sites of contestation, journalists are having to find individual ways of negotiating and disconnecting from the sometimes abusive interactions they experience from audiences. Building on interview data, we explore how journalists have used disconnection practices when systemic organizational support is not available. Finally, we explore how a systemic approach to these issues may be more conducive to the well-being of journalists and propose a few ways forward for the news industry overall. We argue for a systemic approach to support people working in journalism involving a combination of media organizations with education institutions, law enforcement, policy, and regulation.

A Lack of Institutional Support for Disconnection

Whitney Philips argues that commercial media has institutionalized online violence, and this violence has disproportionately affected women and minorities.[10] Despite the rise of online threats to women and minorities around the world, we know little about the resources or programs news organizations have put in place to support journalists.[11] Increasing professionalization of social media cultures of sharing has created forms of social media fatigue and dissatisfaction for many journalists. While many have expressed alarm at the rise in online harassment, others have expressed frustration with increased affective labor, dissatisfaction with the communication culture on particular social media platforms, and increased anxiety about the possible impact of social media use on their professional reputation or personal well-being.[12] Despite this, rising expectations to connect with peers and audiences on social media continue to mark modern newsrooms. Journalists have responded to these expectations and their own frustrations by developing individual disconnection strategies or, in conjunction with the support of civil society and academic organizations, by temporarily disconnecting from journalism, such as through digital forms of disconnection such as resilience training.[13]

The individual development and maintenance of these strategies reveal the lack of support journalists have received from news organizations to adjust to the new and often increased labor associated with being ambiently online. As shown in chapter 4, many of the online and social media policies organizations provide to journalists are focused on issues such as reputation management and risk. Some organizations expect that journalists' adaptation to online and social media labor, including online trolling, abuse, and harassment, is the responsibility of the individual journalist. As maintenance of online professional personas is generally driven by journalists themselves, organizations might leverage the benefits of online engagement but take none of the responsibility for its impacts.

It has generally been left to other organizations to support journalists and advocate for institutional change around online harassment. Journalists have been able to access a coalition of support organizations, including the Committee to Protect Journalists (CPJ) and the IWMF, which launched a digital security hub to provide support and resources to journalists attempting to tackle online abuse.[14] The IWMF Emergency Fund acts as a crisis line for women journalists, and the Journalists in Distress (JID) network offers eighteen international organizations that provide direct assistance to journalists facing online threats.[15] In Nigeria and Ghana, the nonprofit Center for Journalism, Innovation and Development (CJID), along with Free Press Unlimited, offers psychotherapy sessions to assist reporters and media workers who have been exposed to traumatic events.[16]

Other organizations offer services to journalists who may experience harassment or trolling online, one of which is a webinar, offered by TrollBusters, that trains journalists to fight online abuse and develop digital security.[17] TrollBusters most often recommends disconnection strategies for journalists, such as blocking other users, muting or turning off online and social media channels at set times, and blocking, muting, or ignoring perpetrators of online abuse.[18] The latter has become common practice for journalists negotiating various forms of online interaction. Training sessions range from "Defense against the Digital Dark Arts for Journalists," "Physical Security for Journalists," and "Online Security for Journalists." This training teaches journalists about secure browsing tools, digital footprint monitoring, encryption communication, third-party apps, and permissions to ensure that journalists' online labor is not preyed upon by trolls and abusers. The Canadian Journalism Forum on Violence and Trauma helps the physical and emotional safety of journalists in Canada and abroad by serving as a hub through training, news and publications, and workshops.[19] Industry leaders such as the International Press Institute and Poynter also offer lists of resources and tips, from employee assistance programs to meditation and mindfulness applications to community efforts, as a way to reconnect with their work.[20] While this training is useful, it nonetheless places the responsibility of engaging with such resources and on enacting protections on individual journalists.

Taking a more institutional approach, the Dart Center for Journalism and Trauma, based at the Columbia University Graduate School of Journalism, has long been a leader in the field, especially when it comes to offering service on journalism and trauma. In 2020 the Dart Centre Europe, along with the International Press Institute, fostered spaces to discuss and develop a set of measures that newsrooms and journalists could use to prevent and/or minimize the emotional stress and trauma related to online harassment. Such efforts included strategies to implement peer-support networks, reduce the profession's exposure to violent content, and develop self-care plans for journalists in newsrooms. This approach highlights that efforts to train journalists have been a burden carried at the community level. It is imperative that news organizations that do not adopt a systemic approach to harassment create a culture of safety for online engagement and create clearer steps and resources to disconnect from and report harassment and abuse.

Disconnection Tactics to Cope with Online Harassment

Some organizations have provided resources for workforce management to facilitate change within to support the well-being of employees. Examples include rotating teams on and off traumatic stories and comment moderation labor to give journalists time to decompress between tasks. News organizations have also provided physical spaces of empathy for journalists in editorial meetings to share and speak about their experiences with mental health.[21] Larger organizations like the *Wall Street Journal* and Reuters provide courses to support the mental health and well-being of journalists. The Reuters and Facebook Journalism Project courses help journalists to identify and tackle manipulated media online, including abusive content.[22] In the weeks following the 2016 US presidential election, BuzzFeed Open Lab and OpenNews—a network that seeks to connect developers, designers, journalists, and editors to collaborate on open technologies and processes within journalism—assembled a series of training modules and resource guides to help people step up their security literacy.[23] News organizations in Latin America and across the world have started hiring in-house therapists to support their staff.[24]

Despite this, our interview-based study of thirty-four journalists found that efforts led by organizations were focused on individual experiences of acute harassment rather than on developing systemic solutions.[25] Organizations were perceived to largely assume that journalists should know what to do online, that all online interaction with audiences will be productive, and that online harassment is rare and easily dealt with. As one journalist suggested, "Connect, connect, connect. We hear that every week at our newsroom [meetings]. We hear all the numbers on how we are or aren't hitting our marks with connection. But as soon as we say, 'Hey, so and so said some awful shit this week about us on Facebook,' the conversation ends. Nothing. Back to connect."[26]

As a result, organizational policy for online interactions has focused on policing journalists' own behavior online rather than creating resources for negative or unwanted interactions with online audiences.[27] When journalists in our study reported experiencing harassment, whether minor or acute, they said that newsroom managerial action was often dismissive and unbalanced. As a male journalist said, "We're just expected to take care of ourselves. We know what we're getting into and raising red flags all the time doesn't help anyone."[28]

Journalists said they were worried about being stigmatized as incapable of doing their jobs if they discussed harassment and its resulting impact. They knew that if they did discuss it, they would just be pointed to human resources or their insurance for therapy options. Journalists also reported feeling alienated in the newsroom or a sense of shame for not simply dealing with abuse. One journalist said:

> When you're out here on your own it's sort of like, well, what's another thing they want me to do on my own? Figure out what to do with social media without looking like an idiot, without offending readers, and without violating any unwritten rules they have. And when things fall apart and people start coming for my head, well, it's just me. No one's there to report to. Maybe human resources, but how are they going to call the guy who is tweeting me about knowing what kind of car I drive? Or the other guy who keeps hash tagging me about Jesus knowing my sins? They can't do anything, and they won't. Just out here on my own, and that starts to take a toll.[29]

When reporting chronic and escalatory harassment, journalists said they did so cautiously, with anxiety about being labeled "emotionally unsure" or causing unnecessary concern within their news organizations. Journalists were not clear whom to initially report harassment to, though they said that if they had reported harassment or had thought about reporting harassment, their editors were their first option. Journalists indicated that their editors took such reports seriously, referring them to human resources or legal resources within the organization. Journalists said their editors followed up with them, and they discussed ways to avoid or address such harassment after it was reported. Those approaches were predominantly at the individual level, even when human resources became involved. While a few journalists reported being asked what they did wrong, they were told the harassment was not their fault. It was, though, their problem. One journalist said: "Just tell me who to talk to or where to go to deal with this. I don't care if it's even [the news organization] saying, 'We're not equipped for this, but tell us what happened so we can help.'"[30] And another said, "If [the news organization] will take such a hard line on race discrimination or sexual harassment in house, where's the support when we're out in it? I get that it's easier to police your own, but that doesn't mean you just decide to shrug when we're here telling you more every day that we need help."[31] All these responses put journalists at both professional and personal risk of poor mental and physical health outcomes or even burnout (see chapter 3).[32] These health impacts included reports of unhealthy coping practices, such as drinking, overeating, and other types of stress-related activities. As one journalist noted, "If they [my news organization] tells me to handle it, I'll handle it with a long run and a beer after."[33]

Journalists also responded to harassment in online and social media spaces with disconnection practices. Journalists said they took social media breaks fairly frequently. They noted that disconnecting from social media, whether for set dates and times or just to take a breather, helped them to recenter themselves and to engage less reactively. But without a safety net or a barrier provided by their organizations, journalists returned to social media with hesitancy and fear. As an example, a self-described introverted journalist said that "it was either let the harassment consume me little by little over time or do something about it. Not considering how I like to spend my own time, our [human resources director] gave me information about local meetup groups. . . . I felt dismissed and discouraged, so I started watching more Netflix instead."[34] In terms of harassment on social media platforms, journalists said they also talk among themselves about ways to curb harassment before it starts. Journalists said that while they did feel some sense of relief when sharing their experiences with others who had experienced harassment, they felt increasing anxiety and mental and emotional unrest when faced with escalatory harassment.

In our interviews, journalists did not mention training or preventative measures against online harassment beyond the typical human resource information regarding harassment within the organization. The lack of systematic effort, whether experienced or perceived, led journalists to say that they found themselves more frequently considering ways to disconnect from social media platforms altogether. These techniques included seeking stories that required more time away from social media or turning away from social media interaction at night. They also said they found ways to take small breaks from social media that weren't noticeable by their news organizations, which usually entailed not using platforms for a few hours at a time or only using their more personal or private accounts. A journalist said she had received support for disconnecting from her editor: "She seemed to get it and told me to be sure I stepped out of the fire when I needed to."[35]

Other research showed that a number of forms of self-censorship, including avoiding covering certain stories, or being more careful in framing reportage were common approaches to avoiding online harassment.[36] Technology journalists in the United States have said that they purposely disguised their identity and gender or published work anonymously to avoid harassment in the male-dominated technology media field.[37] Cross-cultural research showed that limiting exposure to social media, changing the stories they reported on, and using technological tools to prevent abuse were typical disconnection behaviors used by journalists globally.[38] Some cultural differences existed in expected tolerance of harassment: some journalists were expected to be "strong like a man," while others were more likely to report abuse to police or limit social media use altogether.[39]

Our interviews confirmed that these individual approaches also prevail in newsroom management. The organizational responses journalists discussed during interviews favored an individual approach such as self-care activities while not seeking to address the harassment systemically. To address chronic and escalatory harassment, organizations offered journalists a number of prescriptive and individual solutions. These included ignoring the harassment or harasser(s); engaging in a less defensive manner; countering with positive comments or humor; reporting the harassment to the social media platform by filing a report; talking to other journalists who had experienced harassment; decreasing stress through yoga, running, or meditation; and seeking mental health resources through insurance provided by the organization.

Journalists who used these coping mechanisms still reported increased anxiety and uncertainty related to their jobs. They cited mounting pressures to produce more content, to engage audiences across social media platforms, and to take on more online roles to go alongside their reporting, such as going live on Facebook or Instagram. In other research, journalists indicated that they were more acutely aware of organizational policies and pressures to ensure that they were posting regularly and felt compelled to continue with online work despite its negative impacts. For example, many journalists chose professional interactions according to a particular social media platform and its perceived communication culture. Journalists reported separating personal and professional interactions onto specific platforms, such as using a public profile on Twitter to disseminate professional work and a closed and private profile on Instagram to keep up with family and friends, depending on whether certain organizational policies precluded journalists from having personal social media (see chapter 4).

Other journalists interviewed said they had made strategic decisions to prioritize different social media platforms according to how they articulated their own professional norms into a social media communication style. One journalist explained that they had developed a strong sense of community on Instagram that differed from their experience on other platforms. Thus, disconnection strategies emerged, from brief time-based strategies to more focused professionalization of online practices that allow journalists to connect online without disconnecting from journalism altogether.[40]

Systemic Approaches to Online Harassment: A Way Forward

Lack of systemic preventative efforts from news organizations, such as internal policies, procedures, training, and education, has led journalists to perceive that they have little support to tackle online harassment and has resulted in an undeniable chilling effect on how BIPOC and female journalists are able to do their jobs. There is certainly no single solution to tackle issues of online abuse and harassment. Some solutions may not be scalable, and others require investment of time, effort, and financial resources, all things that are scarce in the current news industry's precarious environment. They can all afford a similar set of principles that are geared to taking an empathetic and humanizing approach to digital labor rather than one focused on the bottom line. In reaction to the resignation of two of its newly appointed leaders due to alleged work pressures, Evan Smith, founder of the *Texas Tribune*, echoed these concerns: "I think that the culture of this place and the degree to which the normal work that we take on has an adverse effect on the lives and well-being of people is something that we have to confront as an organization. Not just us as an organization, but us as an industry."[41]

In our interviews, journalists said they believed that understanding what harassment looks like in its many forms and how to handle it individually and within their news organization before they encountered harassment would alleviate some of their concern about the impact of abuse. Without such resources in place, journalists said that knowing that their news organizations would "take a stand for me," as one journalist said, would also provide a level of assurance. Similarly, having mental health resources readily available at organizations "and not just after a big fire or a building collapses or someone dies," as one journalist said, was mentioned as one systemic change news organizations could make. Another was making it clear who was available to talk to about professional preventative measures to address harassment.

Building on our interviews and amplifying research that has been established in practice, we suggest two approaches to harassment of journalists.[42] First, news organizations should act with empathetic leadership by providing spaces for connection and collaboration on solutions. Second, along with other societal actors, including platform companies and civil society and nonprofit organizations, organizations should adopt a systemic approach to supporting journalists beyond individual approaches.

Most news organizations can improve journalists' working experience by accepting and recognizing the added burden on digital work and the inequalities resulting from it. Considering the human side of social news engagement means making room for different people and their different needs, from student journalists, managers, and editors to senior, midcareer, or junior reporters.[43] As harassment can affect people in very personal ways, news organizations should consider developing industry standards and operating procedures to assess and respond to the risk of emotional and physical attacks on journalists. The Dart Center developed a standard procedure, particularly for offensive and graphic user-generated content, with a "series of structured steps for how to craft a personalized workflow for handling graphic content that depicts death, injury, and other violations."[44]

While operating procedures enable a systemic approach to harassment, organizational acknowledgment of the often personalized and discriminatory nature of harassment is also essential. Practitioners and managers also need to understand the impact that gender, race, and sexuality have on the physical and emotional well-being of digital workers. Our research shows that those who identify as women, people of color, and LGBTQIA+ communities are most negatively affected by harassment on social media. Such work conditions have an impact on retention, as we have seen journalists, mostly women and people of color and especially in the United States, leave the profession altogether.

A way to improve both retention and amplification of diverse journalistic voices is to dismantle the systems that dehumanize needs for support in doing the labor of journalism.[45] Normalizing and humanizing individual and group support processes for journalists is essential to this process. These processes should enable support networks, such as group chats, with options for anonymity and formality. These could include brief and informal conversations, spaces dedicated to support and conversation, all the way through to formal digital mentoring and systems to document and track reported cases of harassment for follow-up with police or other services.

These changes require media organizations to therefore adopt a systemic approach to supporting journalists beyond associations and individual approaches. While individual and community approaches to online harassment are useful in raising awareness and providing tools and a community to discuss issues related to the labor of journalism, they do not provide opportunity for a broader culture shift in newsrooms.

A systemic approach means developing mechanisms to change the culture of the organization. These are reflected in clear policies, support mechanisms, and awareness training sessions that are centralized in their approach. More organizational approaches to responding to and thwarting online harassment would also mean training managerial staff to use safety contact lists, performance checklists, and archives as part of operational procedures. Management of staff might also include regular discussions in editorial meetings or memos and normalization of mental and physical well-being checks, establishing a culture of discussion and an exchange of tactics for healthy connection and disconnection online.

Furthermore, the escalatory nature of some online harassment requires more formal support mechanisms within news organizations that would be part of this systemic change. These supports could include digital security assessment and support, legal support, and, in the case of physical threats, potential relocation or reassignment without professional or financial impact on the journalist. Training in awareness, risk management, and digital security is an essential part of the culture of the organization and can be gained in various manners and understandings of the structural inequalities embedded in online connective practices. Reuters uses the services of CiC Global counseling services, an employee assistance program provider, to develop training, a global trauma hotline, and a support group for its employees and alumni, Peer Network.[46]

Much of this approach is about changing the systemic culture of newsrooms that treats journalists as a potential risk or financial liability and instead humanizes their labor and experience of online communication environments. Many of the journalists we spoke to said that young reporters were being burned out before they even got a chance to develop a professional career. If the individual digital labor of journalists is being leveraged by news organizations to bring increasingly diversified audiences to news, these organizations also bear responsibility for ensuring a culture that allows protection, development, and sharing of these individual skills and labor.

Changing systemic culture also means that organizations better advocate for the safety of professional journalistic practice at an institutional level. While voices such as Taylor Lorenz have called for broader institutional protections for journalists representing diverse and minority stories, broader change is required. Large news organizations and social media platforms could work collaboratively toward governance that protects journalism, but the focus thus far has largely been about getting platforms to pay for social media content. The conditions in which journalism is made matter, especially in nations where free speech is not protected and journalists cannot advocate for themselves. This highlights the need for news organizations to be part of the call for new regulatory and normative operational responses to ensure both protection and amplification of journalistic freedoms.

At a time when journalists, including women, BIPOC, and LGBTQIA+ communities, are experiencing increased forms of harassment and threats online and on social media, the question remains as to how news organizations are providing support to their employees. The examples in this chapter show that these journalists still need to connect online despite the harassment that they experience on social media. While disconnection strategies like the ones discussed in this chapter and throughout this book show some of the ways journalists deal with the pressures of constant connectivity, we also acknowledge the need for lasting organizational and institutional changes in journalism.

The problems experienced by journalists are systemic, part of larger social and cultural problems related to social media platforms, policies, legal systems, and expectations in institutions of education and workplaces.[47] A systemic approach to solving those issues not only involves the workplace but also needs "buy-in from platform companies to respond more effectively and strategically for online violence in order to support and protect their female [and minority] content makers; for law and order bodies to respond with regulatory and policing strategies tailored to discourage it; and for educators to prepare their students to combat it."[48] In combination, more research into systemic work on institutional responses is needed.

As Diana Bossio and Avery Holton suggest, journalists have renegotiated "professional and personal boundaries around journalists' social media use, influenced by the technological, social, and cultural affordances of specific media platforms, organizational and institutional constraints, as well as the online literacies and behaviors of journalists themselves."[49] Journalists and their news organizations in turn must bring those skills and experiences toward systemic change in empathetic and humanized news cultures. This would undoubtedly be the start of transitioning a news industry in turmoil into a workplace that develops safe, trusted, and connected online professional practices in combination with social media platforms and policies, civil society, educators, researchers, and legal and policy systems. For that, we need to consider disconnection practices as part of a systemic approach to the mental health and well-being of journalists and disconnection as part of the contemporary labor of journalism.

Conclusion

One of the key questions for contemporary journalists is how to report in ways that are relevant, trusted, and useful in an age of digital changes and innovation, shrinking newsrooms, and dispersed and varied audiences. With the number of sources of news and information constantly growing, journalists have struggled to adapt their practice to new technologies, new forms of audience connection, and new ways to present their work. In doing so, journalists have sought to harness digital and social media environments prioritizing communication cultures of openness, transparency, and collaboration with audiences and have generated innovative news practices, for better or worse. There have been collaborations with social media audiences from reporting the Arab Spring on Twitter to Chinese journalists' use of WeChat to expose the initial spread of COVID-19 to media colleagues around the world.[1] Practices related to social media logics, including personal branding, content commercialization, influence, and attention strategies, have also challenged journalists personally and professionally, from the lack of clear social media policies to online harassment. The ongoing development and integration of these practices and cultures produce unique impacts on news organizations, the profession, and journalists.

Given the profound impact digital transformation has had on journalists, this book aimed to refocus this key question: How can the news industry support the everyday work of journalists to uphold the practices, norms, and ideals of high-quality, critical, and engaged journalism?

Throughout the book we have shown that journalists are frustrated with the lack of support for their work and well-being. News organizations ask journalists to "live online." At the same time, they ask journalists to "use their health insurance for counseling" if they suffer online harassment in the course of their work.[2] Organizations suggest to journalists that the negative outcomes of their online engagement are a personal responsibility and that the positive outcomes of such engagement belong to the organization. These expectations are at best fatiguing for journalists and at worst cause so much stress that journalists leave the industry altogether. These expectations are burning out a generation of journalists at a time when the public desperately needs their skills and the diversity of their critical voices to make informed social and political choices.

For their part, many journalists create connection and disconnection strategies that allow them to better mediate their working life online and make choices that are both professionally productive and personally satisfying. At their heart, disconnection strategies are humanizing: they prioritize empathetic approaches to online practice that acknowledge the difficulties of online engagement while also finding possibility for safety and enjoyment. While most of these strategies are developed by and focus on individual journalists, we believe that a systemic humanizing approach to journalism practice on digital and social media is now needed.

In this concluding chapter, we advocate for journalists, news organizations, and larger media institutions to create a culture of safety for online connection and clearer steps and resources to disconnect from the various impacts of "living online." First, journalism needs to reckon with the pressures contemporary journalists are experiencing and adopt a systemic approach to mental health and well-being. Second and most important, such an approach needs to consider disconnection practices as part of the journalistic labor of connectivity. One of the best ways to support journalists is to provide institutional space for strategic disconnection from social media.

Providing Institutional Spaces for Strategic Disconnection Practices

Research about journalism on online and social media often focuses on connection and community (see chapter 2).[3] But work in this area has recently highlighted journalists' dissatisfaction with platforms, including platform cultures, logics, and the constant demands that being online places on journalists' labor and time.[4] Journalists are encouraged and in some cases required to engage with audiences in an effort to attract attention, but this increased visibility at best creates social pressure to be present and at worst leads to harassment, trolling, and threats, from which journalists understandably want to disconnect. In this book we have argued that the need to disconnect is one of many complex and ongoing strategies that journalists, like all media users, bring to their negotiation of social media in their personal and professional lives.

Disconnection practices, including digital minimalism and digital detox, have become part of the popular culture vernacular people use to talk about their uneasy relationship with social media.[5] In this book we have shown that disconnection has been referred to as a kind of disconnect from the "cultural logic" of connection so often espoused by social media companies and their algorithmic influence on people's lives.[6] Individuals use disconnection strategies to avoid or mediate the connective affordances of social media between and among websites and in relation to a user's offline experience."[7] Disconnection tactics discussed in this book include creating private spheres for interaction, using technical boundaries like blocking and muting, taking micro breaks from digital and social media connections, or turning away from engagement or interaction altogether. Forms of online disconnection have often focused on issues of privacy, surveillance, and reluctance or nonuse of social media.[8]

Following Ben Light's work on disconnection, this book has shown that journalists' methods of disconnecting from professional social media practices work in tandem with the different ways journalists connect online, that is, the way journalists make online and social media work according to their individual professional, organizational, and personal needs.[9] This points to how journalists are changing their labor practices to be more connected online and how different organizational, institutional, and social contexts can impact these practices and journalists.

We have argued that the need to disconnect is one of many complex and ongoing strategies that journalists, like all media users, bring to their negotiation of social media in their personal and professional lives, though we acknowledge that disconnection does not solve all problems of online labor. Instead, disconnection strategies focus on the "mutability" of connection online, creating contexts where sustainable incorporates measured disconnection in professional work to enhance the work experience.[10] It cannot be a single practice, as it constitutes "several active and random disruptions, disengagements and sometimes even accidents that allow connection to be feasible in certain contexts and more sustainable long-term."[11]

In surveying the forms of disconnections journalists deployed to reconnect with their work, we proposed that news organizations should consider providing intentional spaces for journalists to disconnect. These disconnection practices can be linked into workflows. For example, Reuters has been a leader in the field in managing the mental health of employees. Collaborating with CiC, its global counseling service, Reuters has facilitated peer networks for facilitating its employees to talk about trauma and stress. The company has also provided breaks for journalists who came back from the "daily pressure of the job to burnout, depression, anxiety, PTSD or other conditions" related to their work.[12] Yet most of these efforts are often tied to trauma and on-site reporting. The destigmatization, intentionality, and openness to create spaces of disconnection should also apply to online and social media contexts.

A second focal point of the book is journalists' daily practice of news production and how these practices are framed by the negotiation of work structures, professional ideologies, and responses to a changing media context. Issues such as poor organizational policies and support for social media labor, experiences of harassment and abuse online, and even the culture of specific platforms can impact journalistic practices and professional well-being. Alternate forms of connection and disconnection provide journalists options, especially in contexts where social media use is unavoidable but also unsupported. Journalists can attempt to strengthen connections by selectively aiming to control their presence and foster safer spaces for connection.

Tero Karppi also points to the difficulty users have in disconnecting from social media.[13] On the one hand, platform executives understand and position disconnection as an existential threat. They also fight against disconnection with a number of technical tools. In this context, disconnection practices can be an effective force that improves user agency against threats to individual privacy, safety, and labor. These are all indicators of the process of reflection and response to what constitutes the personal, organizational, technological, and institutional contributions to a journalist's professional context.

Disconnection should be understood as an active negotiation of practice, tools, and rules of journalism. These negotiations of disconnection strategies can be productive tensions. From a conceptual and practical standpoint, they at least highlight how journalism, like all communication practices, reflects on and responds to technological changes, as well as the social and cultural changes that emerge alongside them. The expertise or skill of the journalist is thus not always renegotiated in social media environments or the need for professional journalism overall. It could be that forms of disconnections are oriented toward giving news organizations prestige or, more bluntly, to provide them with tools to make journalists more productive and effective at their jobs.

In chapter 2 we explored the impacts of these strategies on journalists' online work, namely, burnout. In focusing on the labor of journalism and the forms of disconnections through personal and professional boundaries on social media, we have been struck by the increasing reports by journalists of fatigue, stress, and mental illness resulting from the amount and type of online connection required by their work.

Many of these approaches to disconnection can seem to conflict with the image of the journalist seen in media and fiction and even within a journalist's own professional self-conception. Those representations, however, rarely deal with the effects of a professional identity focused on twenty-four-hour commitment to news and newsrooms. We thus argue that forms of disconnection from online labor should be routinized and normalized both within media organizations and in journalists' professional labor.

We do not propose turning off or turning away altogether from online work. As the Dart Center suggests, journalists should not be pushed to that point in the first place.[14] Instead, forms of disconnection from online work could be incorporated into daily life , including limiting exposure to distressing images and stories, participating in social activities outside work, and ensuring adequate self-care through attention to sleep, nutrition, and exercise.[15] These new journalistic skills and practices center compassionate, safe, and engaged connections with online audiences.

We have also shown that some journalists have already individually developed those skills and practices. As we argued in chapter 3, "the feeling of exposure and pressure to be constantly available and engaged on social media are ingredients in a recipe for burnout. Thus, the paradox is that the harder organizations push branding, the less their employees will be able to give to all endeavors."[16]

If quality journalism that connects with audiences is the goal of media organizations, then news organizations have had no choice but to center their strategic goals around the individualistic pursuits of journalists on social media. Leveraging the skills and talents of journalists using social media should not simply be an assumed part of their role; rather than exploiting all the work journalists have done to normalize social media practices, these should be part of the ongoing training, resourcing, and development of journalists and of quality reportage.

In chapters 3 and 4 we began to work through some of these individual practices of connection and disconnection and their impacts on journalists' online work. In chapter 3 we showed how journalists have used personal branding as a commercialized process of connection on social media. We presented a series of tensions in norms and values that branding creates, most notably, between individual journalists and the organizations they work for. These tensions become more difficult to navigate as both journalists and organizations respond to technological and cultural changes and try to uphold their own professional ideals.[17] Organizations have responded with policies that often leave journalists confused and undersupported as they navigate shifting terrain online.

We explored some of the impacts of this in chapter 5, where we showed that COVID-19 misinformation and disinformation on social media point to larger issues surrounding the changing modes of connection between journalists and audiences and the disconnection from broader social norms around journalism's professional ideologies. We argued that misinformation and disinformation about the COVID-19 pandemic and vaccine point to larger disagreements over which sources of information should be trusted and considered relevant on social media.

As a result, we saw media organizations and individual journalists thinking very carefully about connection practices that highlight good-quality journalism in environments already polluted with misinformation. The strategies and skills that we described in these chapters point to important questions. First, they point to a question related to the value proposition that professional journalism brings to online audiences. Second, they direct us to ask how to present this value to audiences who are increasingly distrustful, distracted, or even just ambivalent about the relevance of journalism in their informational diet.

Finally, in chapter 6 we came back to the impacts of underdeveloped institutional and organizational structures for online professional labor on journalists using the case of online abuse and harassment. While much of the impact of social media work has been felt through the physical and mental well-being of the journalists, it was important to acknowledge the important risks journalists may encounter in their online work.

While this book in part focuses on connection and disconnection in the context of personal and professional branding, misinformation, newsroom policy, and online harassment, we acknowledge that there are many other ways academic research has addressed the challenges journalists face in a time of digital transformation, including through precarity, trauma and mental health, and digital security.[18] This book has been our attempt to bring some of these issues together under a unified conceptual framework, though there is of course, more to research and more change to advocate for.

Toward Understanding Contemporary Journalism through Disconnection

News and media organizations have much to lose by not investing in the professional practices that support the institutional ideals of quality journalism and forms of disconnections. Such impact can surface in retention issues in newsrooms. Research is showing that journalists are increasingly leaving the profession. Journalist Elizabeth Djinis wrote in *Poynter* that leaving professional journalism to pursue freelance writing was a decision that empowered her both mentally and financially: "By going out on my own, I've come into my own. I've started to realize who I am and who I want to be as a writer and a professional."[19]

Freelance work doesn't suit all workers, but there are several other fields that value journalistic skills and have many more beneficial remuneration and development opportunities. This isn't necessarily a new development in a digitally converged environment. What is new, however, is that increasingly journalists are being asked to support their professional ideals and public service with increasingly risky labor, public, unsupported, and individual labor that actively harms their mental and physical health.

Journalists have been hinting at these risks for some time. They are asked to make risky experiments in online and social media publishing and community engagement. But they are also often publicly paying for those risks if those experiments go awry. Other journalists have pointed to the strain of shrinking newsrooms, of 24–7 news cycles, of precarious labor, and of taking online labor into their personal lives with little organizational resourcing or mental health support. In this context, it is unsurprising that journalists are embracing what previously would have been seen as the precarious labor of freelancing.

Research has shown that these impacts result from the financial devastation that has been pushed on newsrooms with digital disruption and increasing platformization of content. But funding is not the only issue, nor is it the only answer. Our exploration of some of the connection and disconnection practices journalists use shows that these skills exist and are being actively developed by individuals, but they are not organizationally supported or shared. Skill development in creating online communities that are safe and productive is key for improving contemporary professional journalism.

The COVID-19 pandemic has had an impact on journalism, including increasing opportunities for journalists to work autonomously, along with the impacts that continuous online interaction has had on journalists' well-being. The effects of the pandemic on disconnection practices are global. With a rise in the use of smartphones, apps like WhatsApp and Telegram have become especially popular in the Global South, such as Brazil, creating many more dissemination methods for health misinformation to spread.[20] The pandemic has already had important implications for the well-being of journalism, but we need to be attuned more to its effects, especially for the attraction of young talent and the retention of journalists within the field.

The key to safe and consistent organizational approaches to journalism labor lies first in acknowledging that social media engagement practices are a necessary journalistic skill; then in positioning the editorial, relational, and promotional aspects of that labor as part of a journalist's role; and finally in creating spaces that are supportive of developing and sharing those skills with ample time and resourcing. This may seem like a difficult task when the business of news is in turmoil (e.g., a shortage in workforce and retention issues). This approach has had positive consequences within other professions. For example, research about social media workers in mental health communications shows that while funding may influence the amount of content produced, the development of high-quality engagement is linked to professionals who are trained and thus extremely skilled in employing affective labor to "show care" for audiences.[21]

The story of journalists' use of digital, online, and social media has largely been about adaptation, change, and the influence of online cultures on the unique connections that journalists form with their audiences. Part of a journalist's role has always been linked to the possibilities for audience engagement in the news, but this connection has become increasingly complex and paradoxical. Creating spaces for disconnection is not turning away from the connection between journalists and their publics. It is instead enabling new practices of connection that both uphold the ideals of journalism and protect the journalists doing the everyday labor to uphold them.

Notes

Introduction

1. Posetti, "Fighting Back."
2. Reuters, "Who Is Nobel Peace Prize Winner Maria Ressa?"
3. Pickard, "The Misinformation Society."
4. Graves and Shabbir, "Gauging the Global Impacts"; Bebawi and Bossio, *Social Media*.
5. Singer et al., *Participatory Journalism*; Hermida, "Post-publication Gatekeeping."
6. Perreault and Perreault, "Journalists on COVID-19 Journalism."
7. Cherubini, Newman, and Kleis Nielsen, "Changing Newsrooms 2021."
8. Cherubini, Newman, and Kleis Nielson, "Changing Newsrooms 2021."
9. It is worth noting that hybrid reporting is not completely new in the history of journalism. Digital cameras, laptops, smartphones, and other mobile technologies also allowed reporters to do their work from a distance.
10. Torsner, "Increasing Numbers of Physical Attacks."
11. Brennan, *Opting Out of Digital Media*; Selwyn, "Digital Division"; Karppi, *Disconnect*; Docherty, "Facebook's Ideal User."
12. Baym, "The New Shape"; Tufekci, "Grooming."
13. Karppi, "Disconnect Me"; Cassidy, "Social Networking Sites"; Hargittai, "Whose Space?"
14. Light, *Disconnecting*.
15. Hayes, Singer, and Ceppos, "Shifting Roles, Enduring Values."
16. Light, *Disconnecting*.
17. Light and Cassidy, "Strategies for the Suspension."

18. "Journalism Essentials."

19. Deuze, "What Journalism Is (Not)."

20. Zelizer, "Journalists as Interpretive Communities"; Bélair-Gagnon and Horton, "Boundary Work"; Ryfe, "The Ontology of Journalism."

21. Paulussen, "Technology"; Dean, "Communicative Capitalism"; Raun, "Capitalizing Intimacy."

22. boyd and Ellison, "Social Network Sites"; Alejandro, "Journalism."

23. Albarran, *The Social Media Industries.*

24. Treem and Leonardi, "Social Media Use in Organizations."

25. Bossio et al., "Social Media Managers as Intermediaries."

26. Carlson and Lewis, *Boundaries of Journalism*; Deuze, "What Is Journalism?"

27. Deuze, "What Is Journalism?"

28. Carlson, *Journalistic Authority.*

29. Mattar, "Objectivity."

30. Ryfe, *Can Journalism Survive?*; Lowery, "Journalism Innovation"; Nel and Westlund, "The 4C's of Mobile News."

31. Lasorsa, Lewis, and Horton, "Normalizing Twitter."

32. Singer, "The Ethics of Social Journalism."

33. Hermida, "Tweets and Truth"; Hedman, "J-Tweeters"; Bossio and Bebawi, "Mapping the Emergence."

34. Hirst and Treadwell, "Blogs Bother Me."

35. Robinson, "'Journalism as Process'"; Lasorsa, Lewis, and Holton, "Normalizing Twitter"; Pindayi, "Social Media Uses."

36. Lewis and Molyneux, "A Decade of Research."

37. Mellado et al., "The Hybridization of Journalistic Cultures."

38. Pearson, "Nothing about Us."

39. Westlund, "Producer-Centric."

40. Livingston and Asmolov, "Networks"; Hermida, "Tweets and Truth."

41. Bo et al., "For Better or for Worse"; Posetti, "Combating Online Abuse"; Bossio and Holton, "The Identity Dilemma."

42. We supplemented the interviews with previous interviews we conducted in South Africa, Kenya, Canada, China, Hong Kong, Europe, and the UK.

43. Hand, "Visuality in Social Media."

44. Some of this work has been published as individual journal articles.

45. Duffy, *(Not) Getting Paid.*

46. Hedman and Djerf-Pierre, "The Social Journalist."

47. Lasén, "Digital Self-Portraits."

Chapter 1. Journalism and the Paradox of Connection

1. "Infodemic"; anonymized interview participant, online interview by the author, September 9, 2020.

2. Šimunjak, "Pride and Anxiety."

3. Libert, Le Cam, and Domingo, "Belgian Journalists."

4. Boateng and Buatsi, "Face-to-Face with COVID-19."

5. Posetti, Bell, and Brown, *Journalism and the Pandemic*.

6. "Journalists' Mental Health."

7. Jukes, Fowler-Watt, and Rees, "Reporting the Covid-19 Pandemic."

8. *The Guardian* did go on to introduce a weekly digest magazine in 2018 as an additional subscriber benefit.

9. Baym, *Personal Connections*.

10. Harrison and Barthel, "Wielding New Media."

11. Baym and boyd, "Socially Mediated Publicness."

12. Veum, Undrum, and Victoria, "The Selfie."

13. Fairchild, "Building the Authentic Celebrity."

14. Duffy, "The Romance of Work."

15. Leaver, Highfield, and Abidin, *Instagram*.

16. Ardévol and Gómez-Cruz, "Private Body, Public Image."

17. Abidin, "Agentic Cute."

18. Abidin, "Agentic Cute."

19. Senft, "Microcelebrity."

20. Marwick, "Instafame."

21. Marwick, *Status Update*.

22. Tandoc and Vos, "The Journalist Is Marketing"; Hanusch and Bruns, "Journalistic Branding."

23. Dean, "Communicative Capitalism."

24. Gregg, *Work's Intimacy*, 2, 168.

25. Molyneux, Holton, and Lewis, "How Journalists Engage."

26. Anonymized interview participant, online interview by the author, September 12, 2020.

27. Hedman and Djerf-Pierre, "The Social Journalist."

28. Holton and Lewis, "Journalists."

29. Name withheld, Australian journalist, interview conducted in 2020.

30. See also Perreault and Bélair-Gagnon, "The Lifestyle."

31. Beckett and Deuze, "On the Role of Emotion."

32. Bélair-Gagnon, Nelson, and Lewis, "Audience Engagement."

33. Baym, *Playing to the Crowd*.

34. Mellado, Hellmueller, and Donsbach, *Journalistic Role Performance*.

35. Name withheld, Australian journalist, interview conducted in 2019.

36. Name withheld, Australian journalist, interview conducted in 2021.

37. Papadakis, *Computer-Mediated Communities*.

38. Lewis, "Reciprocity."

39. Xu, "Digital Media."

40. Name withheld, Australian journalist, interview conducted in 2021.

41. Name withheld, Australian journalist, interview conducted in 2019.

42. Ferrucci, "Networked."

43. La et al., "Policy Response."

44. Jukes, Fowler-Watt, and Rees, "Reporting the Covid-19 Pandemic."

45. Jukes, Fowler-Watt, and Rees, "Reporting the Covid-19 Pandemic."

46. Dubberley, Griffin, and Bal, "Making Secondary Trauma."

47. Kania-Lundholm, "Why Disconnecting Matters?"

48. "Meta Investor Relations."

49. Viljoen, "The Promise and Limits."

50. Portwood-Stacer, "Media Refusal."

51. Selwyn, "Digital Division."

52. Van Dijk, "Digital Divide Research."

53. Karppi, "Digital Suicide."

54. Kefi and Maar, "The Power of Lurking."

55. Lutz and Hoffman, "The Dark Side."

56. Syvertsen and Enli, "Digital Detox."

57. Syvertsen and Enli, "Digital Detox."

58. Syvertsen, *Digital Detox.*

59. Deuze, "Media Life."

60. Satchell and Dourish, "Beyond the User"; Bossio and Holton, "Burning Out"; Gregg, *Counterproductive.*

61. Light, *Disconnecting.*

62. Light, *Disconnecting*, 156.

63. Karppi et al., "Disconnection."

64. Karppi, *Disconnect.*

Chapter 2. Burning Out, Turning Off, and Disconnecting

1. Pip Courtney, online interview by the author, December 4, 2018.

2. Tandoc and Vos, "The Journalist Is Marketing."

3. Sacco and Bossio, "Don't Tweet This!"; Martin and Murrell, "Negotiating the Conversation."

4. Lasén and Gómez, "Digital Photography."

5. Wells, "ABC Journalist."

6. Bossio and Holton, "Burning Out."

7. Karppi, "Digital Suicide"; Lasén, "Digital Self-Portraits."

8. Portwood-Stacer, "Media Refusal"; Syvertsen, *Media Resistance.*

9. Tong, "The Defence"; Yum, "Beyond Gatekeeping."

10. Terranova, "Free Labor."

11. Qiu, Gregg, and Crawford, "Circuits of Labor."

12. Terranova, "Free Labor." On "immaterial labor," see Brouillette, "Creative Labor." On agreed exchange, see Deuze, "Media Life"; Marwick, *Status Update*; and Duffy, *(Not) Getting Paid.*

13. Maslach and Jackson, "The Measurement."

14. Backholm and Björkqvist, "The Effects"; Jung and Kim, "Causes of Newspaper Firm"; Burke and Matthiesen, "Workaholism."

15. González de Bustamante and Relly, "Journalism."

16. Reinardy, "Newspaper Journalism."

17. MacDonald et al., "Burnout in Journalists."

18. Name withheld, Australian journalist, interview conducted in 2019.

19. Lasén, "Digital Self-Portraits"; Portwood-Stacer, "Media Refusal."

20. Name withheld, Australian journalist, interview conducted in 2019.

21. Light, *Disconnecting*.

22. Light, *Disconnecting*.

23. Light, *Disconnecting*.

24. Light, *Disconnecting*.

25. Light and Cassidy, "Strategies."

26. Light and Cassidy, "Strategies."

27. See Hiltunen, "Trouble in Paradise?"

28. Name withheld, Australian journalist, interview conducted in 2018.

29. Name withheld, Australian journalist, interview conducted in 2018.

30. Coles and West, "Trolling the Trolls"; Lopez, Muldoon, and McKeown, "One Day of #Feminism."

31. Name withheld, Australian journalist, interview conducted in 2018.

32. Name withheld, Australian journalist, interview conducted in 2018.

33. Light and Cassidy, "Strategies."

34. Name withheld, Australian journalist, interview conducted in 2018.

35. Name withheld, Australian journalist, interview conducted in 2019.

36. Name withheld, Australian journalist, interview conducted in 2019.

37. Molyneux, Lewis, and Holton, "Media Work."

38. Name withheld, Australian journalist, interview conducted in 2018.

39. Light and Cassidy, "Strategies."

40. Light, *Disconnecting*.

41. Djerf-Pierre, Ghersetti, and Hedman, "Appropriating Social Media."

42. Djerf-Pierre, Ghersetti, and Hedman, "Appropriating Social Media."

Chapter 3. Maintaining Professional Connections through Branding

1. Chang, "The Substackerati."

2. Chang, "The Substackerati."

3. Jeong, "Casey Newton."

4. Hobbs, "Substack."

5. Allyn, "Tired."

6. Jeong, "Casey Newton."

7. Hobbs, "Substack."

8. Chang, "The Substackerati."

9. Coomber, *Branding*.

10. Jenkins, *Convergence Culture; Livingstone, Audiences and Publics*.

11. Liu, Ainsworth, and Baumeister, "A Meta-analysis."

12. Peters, "The Brand Called You."

13. Murphy, *Branding*.

14. Coomber, *Branding*.

15. Williams, "The Basics of Branding."

16. Kalleberg, "Precarious Work."

17. Kalleberg, "Precarious Work."

18. Grieco, "US Newspapers."

19. Adgate, "Local News."

20. Grieco, "Fast Facts"; Barthel, Matsa, and Worden, "Coronavirus-Driven Downturn."

21. Mahone et al., "Who's Producing Local Journalism?"

22. "World Press Trends."

23. Kalleberg, "Precarious Work."

24. Prassl, Humans as a Service.

25. Collinson, "Identities and Insecurities."

26. Gandini, "Digital Work."

27. Örnebring, "Journalists Thinking"; Deuze and Witschge, *Beyond Journalism*.

28. Prior, "News vs. Entertainment."

29. Park and Kaye, "What's This?"; Gil de Zúñiga, Weeks, and Ardèvol-Abreu, "Effects of the News-Finds-Me Perception"; Fletcher and Nielsen, "Are People Incidentally Exposed."

30. Tandoc and Vos, "The Journalist Is Marketing."

31. Holton, Bélair-Gagnon, and Royal, "The Human Side"; Marwick and boyd, "Networked Privacy"; Papacharissi, "Without You, I'm Nothing."

32. On making reputations tangible, see Gandini, "Digital Work."

33. Klawitter and Hargittai, "'It's Like Learning.'"

34. Duffy et al., "The Nested Precarities."

35. Van Dijck, Poell, and De Waal, *The Platform Society*.

36. Holton and Molyneux, "Identity Lost?"

37. Molyneux, Lewis, and Holton, "Media Work."

38. Bossio, "Journalists on Instagram."

39. Hedman and Djerf-Pierre, "The Social Journalist."

40. Bossio, "Journalists on Instagram."

41. For the use of interviews, see Wang, Huang, and Guo, "Malleable Multiplicity"; for qualitative textual analysis, see Molyneux, "What Journalists Retweet"; for quantitative content analysis, see Molyneux, Holton, and Lewis, "How Journalists Engage"; and for surveys of journalists, see Molyneux, Lewis, and Holton, "Media Work," and Molyneux, "A Personalized Self-Image."

42. Marwick and boyd, "Networked Privacy."

43. Lough, Molyneux, and Holton, "A Clearer Picture."

44. Carpenter, Kanver, and Timmons, "It's about Me"; Wang, Huang, and Guo, "Malleable Multiplicity"; Mellado and Ovando, "How Chilean Journalists."

45. Lough, Molyneux, and Holton, "A Clearer Picture."

46. Lough, Molyneux, and Holton, "A Clearer Picture."

47. Goffman, *The Presentation of Self.*

48. Siraj-Blatchford, "Educational Research and Reform."

49. Holton and Molyneux, "Identity Lost?"

50. Mellado and Hermida, "A Conceptual Framework."

51. Bentivegna and Marchetti, "Journalists at a Crossroads."

52. Bucher and Helmond, "The Affordances."

53. Senft, "Microcelebrity."

54. Bossio, "Journalists on Instagram."

55. Maares and Hanusch, "Exploring the Boundaries."

56. Marwick, "Instafame."

57. Hedman, "Making the Most of Twitter"; Van Zoonen, Verhoeven, and Vliegenthart, "How Employees Use Twitter"; Lee, "'Friending' Journalists."

58. Vallas and Christin, "Work and Identity."

59. Molyneux and Holton, "Media Work."

60. Molyneux, "A Personalized Self-Image."

61. Marwick and boyd, "Networked Privacy"; Marwick and boyd, "I Tweet Honestly"; Papacharissi, "Without You, I'm Nothing."

62. Smith, "Survey Says."

63. Donsbach, "Psychology of News Decisions."

64. Molyneux and Mourão, "Political Journalists' Normalization."

65. Mourão and Molyneux, "Tweeting outside the Lines."

66. Bossetta, "The Digital Architectures."

67. Wang, Huang, and Guo, "Malleable Multiplicity."

68. Kovach and Rosenstiel, *The Elements of Journalism.*

69. Tien Vu, "The Online Audience"; Waddell, "What Does the Crowd Think?"

70. Reese, *The Crisis.*

71. Creech, *Journalism Education*; Creech and Mendelson, "Imagining the Journalist."

72. Powers and Vera-Zambrano, "How Journalists Use Social Media."

73. Nkie Mongo, "The Practice of Envelope Journalism."

74. Patel, "'A Fun Adventure.'"

75. Pelaprat and Brown, "Reciprocity."

76. Bridgen, "Emotional Labour"; Scolere, Pruchniewska, and Duffy, "Constructing."

Chapter 4. Dis/connecting from Policy and Practice

1. Posted May 31, 2020, at https://twitter.com/alexisjreports/status/1267081467731103749?s=20.

2. Maruca, "Post-Gazette Staffers."

3. Arnold, "Am I Biased?"

4. Schneider, "Journalism Outlets."

5. The organizations whose policies could be found online and were included in this chapter's discourse analysis are as follows: *Agence France-Presse*, https://www.afp.com/communication/new-social-media-guidelines.pdf; *Associated Press*, https://www.ap.org/assets/documents/social-media-guidelines_tcm28–9832.pdf; *BuzzFeed*, https://www.buzzfeednews.com/article/shani/the-buzzfeed-editorial-standards-and-ethics-guide; *The Guardian*, https://www.theguardian.com/info/2020/may/29/social-media-best-practice-guidelines-for-freelance-contributors; the *Los Angeles Times*, https://www.latimes.com/local/readers-rep/la-rr-la-times-updates-newsroom-ethics-guidelines-20140618-story.html; the *New York Times*, https://www.ny-times.com/editorial-standards/social-media-guidelines.html; National Public Radio (NPR), https://www.npr.org/about-npr/688418842/special-section-social-media; the *South China Morning Post*, https://www.scmp.com/policies-and-standards#hoaxes-guidelines?module=inline&pgtype=article; *USA Today*, https://training.usatodaynet-work.com/wp-content/uploads/2020/08/SocialMediaGuidanceforNewsrooms.pdf; and the *Washington Post*, https://www.washingtonpost.com/policies-and-standards/.

6. Vaast and Kaganer, "Social Media Affordances"; Six and Sorge, "Creating a High-Trust Organization."

7. Foote et al., "Employee Commitment."

8. Kane et al., "Community Relations 2.0."

9. Grover, "Fair Workplace Regulation."

10. Arnesen and Weis, "Developing"; Straub et al., "Effective HR Implementation."

11. Klaas and Wheeler, "Managerial Decision Making."

12. Opgenhaffen and Scheerlinck, "Social Media Guidelines."

13. Adornato and Lysak, "You Can't Post That!"

14. Harlow, "Protecting News Companies."

15. Opgenhaffen and Scheerlinck, "Social Media Guidelines."

16. Sacco and Bossio, "Don't Tweet This!"

17. "Social Media Guidelines."

18. Opgenhaffen and Scheerlinck, "Social Media Guidelines."

19. Jian and Liu, "Journalist Social Media Practice."

20. Lee, "Opportunity or Risk?"

21. Holton and Molyneux, "Identity Lost?"; Walters, "Reclaiming Control."

22. Breed, "Social Control"; Currie Sivek, "Social Media."

23. Bossio and Sacco, "From 'Selfies,'" 537.

24. "Social Media Guidelines."

25. Peters, "Lawsuits."

26. "Social Media Guidelines."

27. Marwick and boyd, "Networked Privacy."

28. Lee, "'Friending' Journalists."

29. On criticism of other journalists, see Robertson, "Reporter Felicia Sonmez."

30. Holton et al., "'Not Their Fault.'"

31. Mossberger, Tolbert, and McNeal, *Digital Citizenship*.

32. McCosker and Johns, "Contested Publics."

33. For the two sets of logics, see Bélair-Gagnon, Lewis, and Agur, "Failure to Launch"; on editorial logic, see Fincham, "Business as Usual."

34. Chadwick, *The Hybrid Media System*.

35. Papacharissi, "Without You, I'm Nothing."

36. Papacharissi, *Affective Publics*; Berger and Milkman, "What Makes Online Content Viral?"; Stieglitz and Dang-Xuan, "Emotions."

37. Holton and Molyneux, "Identity Lost?"

38. Patel, "'A Fun Adventure.'"

39. Hermida, "Twitter."

40. Park and Kaye, "What's This?"

41. On acting as a guest, see "Special Section"; on working as a stagehand, see "Policies and Standards."

42. "Social Media Guidelines."

43. Ingram, "Social Media Crackdowns"; Karlsson, "Dispersing."

44. Schiffrin, "Credibility."

45. Grover, "Fair Workplace Regulation."

46. Tormoen, "Champions of Change."

Chapter 5. Connecting with Journalism in an Era of Misinformation

1. Saunokonoko, "Not a Race?"

2. "Vaccine Hesitancy Tracker"; "What's Gone Wrong?"

3. Freelon et al., "Black Trolls Matter."

4. Foa and Mounk, "The Danger of Deconsolidation."

5. Mitchell and Liedke, "About Four in Ten Americans"; Shearer, "Local News."

6. Park et al., "Digital News Report."

7. Watkins et al., "Digital News Report."

8. Fisher, "The Trouble with 'Trust.'"

9. Wihbey et al., "The Bipartisan Case."

10. Nelson and Lewis, "Only 'Sheep' Trust Journalists?"

11. Nelson and Lewis, "Only 'Sheep' Trust Journalists?"

12. Staender et al., "Is Sensationalist Disinformation More Effective?"

13. Van Bavel et al., "Political Psychology."

14. Mourão and Robertson, "Fake News."

15. Mourão and Robertson, "Fake News."

16. Neyazi, Kalogeropoulos, and Nielsen, "Misinformation Concerns"; Valenzuela, Bachmann, and Bargsted, "The Personal."

17. Messing and Westwood, "Selective Exposure."

18. Kirpal and Brown, "The Much Vaunted 'Flexible Employee.'"

19. Wihbey, Twitter, September 18, 2021.

20. Dalzell, "Australia Signs Deals."

21. Taylor, "From 'It's Not a Race.'"
22. Harvey, Koloff, and Wiggins, "How Australia's COVID Vaccine Rollout."
23. "ATAGI Advice."
24. *Herald Sun*, "Today's Front Page."
25. Gubana and Perpitch, "WA Health Authorities."
26. Clun, Cunningham, and Estcourt, "Doctors Warn."
27. Mihailidis and Viotty, "Spreadable Spectacle."
28. Mitra and Pennebaker, "Understanding Anti-Vaccination Attitudes."
29. Anna Rose's handle is no longer active, as she was banned from posting on Instagram in 2021.
30. Bauer, "As a Virologist."
31. Bauer, "As a Virologist."
32. Abidin, "L8r H8r."
33. Abidin, "L8r H8r."
34. Bossio and Sacco, "Defamation."
35. Siguru, "Prophets without Honor."
36. Marwick, Status Update.
37. Duffy, "The Romance of Work."
38. Bossio and Holton, "The Identity Dilemma."
39. Sharnelle Vella, personal interview, 2021.
40. McMahon, "Five Welcome Voices."
41. Sharnelle Vella, personal interview, 2021.
42. Sharnelle Vella, personal interview, 2021.
43. Sharnelle Vella, personal interview, 2021.
44. Solutions or constructive journalism is defined as an approach reportage that focuses on responses to social issues and is anchored in evidence that shows how and why responses can work.
45. Mia Malan, personal interview, 2021.
46. Menezes et al., "What Is Driving."
47. Africa CDC, COVID 19 Vaccine Perceptions.
48. Burger et al., "Increased Openness."
49. Mia Malan, personal interview, 2021.
50. Mia Malan, personal interview, 2021.
51. Mellado and Hermida, "A Conceptual Framework."

Chapter 6. Harassment and Disconnection in Journalism's Digital Labor

1. International Women Media Foundation, "IWMF Condemns Online Attacks against Taylor Lorenz," https://www.iwmf.org/2021/03/iwmf-condemns-online-attacks-against-taylor-lorenz.
2. Waisbord, "Mob Censorship." See also Jamil, "Suffering in Silence"; and Koirala, "Female Journalists' Experience."

3. Jones, "NBC News Defends."
4. Philips, *This Is Why*.
5. Posetti, "The New Frontline."
6. Posetti et al., *The Chilling*.
7. Sales, "Bullying on Twitter."
8. "Impact of COVID19."
9. Adams, "'They Go for Gender First.'"
10. Philips, *This Is Why*.
11. Walsh, Saady, and Martin, "Why Do We Have to Search?"
12. Bossio and Holton, "Burning Out."
13. Holton et al., "'Not Their Fault.'"
14. Sullivan, "Online Harassment."
15. "Workers' Rights."
16. Jamiu, "This Organization."
17. Ferrier and Garud-Patkar, "TrollBusters."
18. "Reporters Exposed."
19. "Promoting the Physical and Emotional Safety."
20. "IPI Launches New Video"; Cobham, "How Journalists Can Take Care."
21. Strom, "It's Time."
22. "Identifying and Tackling."
23. "The Field Guide."
24. Mioli, "Mental Health."
25. Holton et al., "'Not Their Fault.'"
26. Holton et al., "'Not Their Fault.'"
27. Sacco and Bossio, "Don't Tweet This!"
28. Holton et al., "'Not Their Fault.'"
29. Holton et al., "'Not Their Fault.'"
30. Holton et al., "'Not Their Fault.'"
31. Holton et al., "'Not Their Fault.'"
32. Ferrier and Garud-Patkar, "TrollBusters."
33. Holton et al., "'Not Their Fault.'"
34. Holton et al., "'Not Their Fault.'"
35. Holton et al., "'Not Their Fault.'"
36. Binns, "Fair Game?"
37. Adams, "'They Go for Gender First.'"
38. Masullo Chen et al., "'You Really Have.'"
39. Koirala, "Female Journalists' Experience."
40. Mathews, Bélair-Gagnon, and Carlson, "'Why I Quit.'"
41. Robertson, "Two Texas Tribune Leaders."
42. Dubberley and Grant, "Journalism and Vicarious Trauma."
43. Holton, Bélair-Gagnon, and Royal, "The Human Side."

44. Rees, "Handling Traumatic Imagery."
45. Headlines' network for improving mental health in the media pilot project was supported by the Google News Initiative and launched in late 2021. It included interactive workshops for UK journalists across the industry from entry level to senior management.
46. "Creating Global Wellbeing"; Yates, "Burying Mental Health Stigma."
47. "We Belong Here."
48. Martin, "Tackling Gendered Violence," 74.
49. Bossio and Holton, "Burning Out."

Conclusion

1. Hermida, Lewis, and Zamith, "Sourcing the Arab Spring"; Zhang and Wang, "Refracting the Pandemic."
2. Holton et al., "'Not Their Fault.'"
3. Hermida, Lewis, and Zamith, "Sourcing the Arab Spring."
4. Holton et al., "'Not Their Fault.'"
5. Newport, *Digital Minimalism*.
6. Karppi, *Disconnect*.
7. Light, *Disconnecting*.
8. Tufekci, "Grooming."
9. Light, *Disconnecting*.
10. Chia, Jorge, and Karppi, *Reckoning with Social Media*.
11. Bélair-Gagnon et al., "Disconnection."
12. Yates, "Burying Mental Health Stigma."
13. Karppi, *Disconnect*.
14. Bedai, "Taking Time Off."
15. Bedai, "Taking Time Off."
16. Bedai, "Taking Time Off."
17. Molyneux and Holton, "Branding (Health) Journalism"; Hedman, "J-Tweeters."
18. Deuze and Witschge, *Beyond Journalism*; Seely, "Journalists and Mental Health"; Henrichsen, "Understanding Nascent Newsroom Security."
19. Djinis, "Why Are Journalists Leaving."
20. Newman et al., "Digital News Report 2021."
21. Davis, "Examining the Digital Labor."

Bibliography

Abidin, Crystal. "Agentic Cute (^.^): Pastiching East Asian Cute in Influencer Commerce." *East Asian Journal of Popular Culture* 2, no. 1 (2016): 33–47.

Abidin, Crystal. "L8r H8r: Commoditized Privacy, Influencer Wars, and Productive Disorder in the Influencer Industry." In *Produsing Theory in a Digital World 2.0: The Intersection of Audiences and Production in Contemporary Theory: Volume 3*, edited by Rebecca Ann Lind, 31–48. New York: Peter Lang, 2021.

Adams, Catherine. "'They Go for Gender First': The Nature and Effect of Sexist Abuse of Female Technology Journalists." *Journalism Practice* 12, no. 7 (2018): 850–69.

Adgate, Brad. "Local News Losing Billions in Revenue Each Year from Digital Media Giants." *Forbes*, May 17, 2021. https://www.forbes.com/sites/bradadgate/2021/05/17/local-news-losing-billions-in-revenue-each-year-from-digital-media/?sh=601836fd474f.

Adornato, Anthony C., and Suzanne Lysak. "You Can't Post That! Social Media Policies in US Television Newsrooms." *Electronic News*, June 22, 2017, 80–99.

Africa CDC. *COVID 19 Vaccine Perceptions: A 15 Country Study*. March 10, 2020. https://africacdc.org/download/covid-19-vaccine-perceptions-a-15-country-study/.

Ahmed Neyazi, Taberez, Antonis Kalogeropoulos, and Rasmus K. Nielsen. "Misinformation Concerns and Online News Participation among Internet Users in India." *Social Media + Society* 7, no. 2 (2021). https://doi.org/10.117/20563051211009013.

Albarran, Alan B. *The Social Media Industries*. London: Routledge, 2013.

Alejandro, Jennifer. "Journalism in the Age of Social Media." Reuters Institute Fellowship Paper, University of Oxford, 2010, 1. https://www.mediaforum.md/upload/theme-files/journalism-in-the-age-of-social-mediapdf-554fbf10114c6.pdf.

Allyn, Bobby. "Tired of the Social Media Rat Race, Journalists Move to Writing Substack Newsletters." *NPR*, December 2, 2020. https://www.npr.org/2020/12/02/941020719/tired-of-the-social-media-rat-race-journalists-move-to-writing-substack-newslett.

Ardévol, Elisenda, and Edgar Gómez-Cruz. "Private Body, Public Image: Self-Portrait in the Practice of Digital Photography." *Revista de Dialectología y Tradiciones Populares* 67, no. 1 (2012): 181–208.

Arnesen, David W., and William L. Weis. "Developing an Effective Company Policy for Employee Internet and Email Use." *Journal of Organizational Culture, Communications and Conflict* 11, no. 2 (2007): 53–65.

Arnold, Amanda. "Am I Biased Because I'm Black?" *The Cut*, June 15, 2020. https://www.thecut.com/2020/06/black-reporter-barred-from-covering-blm-protests-over-bias.html.

"ATAGI Advice on COVID-19 AstraZeneca (Vaxzevria) Vaccine." Australian Government Department of Health, 2021. https://www.health.gov.au/initiatives-and-programs/covid-19vaccines/learn-about-covid-19-vaccines/about-the-astrazeneca-vaxzevria-covid-19vaccine#thrombosis-with-thrombocytopenia-syndrome-tts.

Backholm, Klas, and Kaj Björkqvist. "The Effects of Exposure to Crisis on Well-Being of Journalists: A Study of Crisis-Related Factors Predicting Psychological Health in a Sample of Finnish Journalists." *Media, War & Conflict* 3, no. 2 (July 2010): 138–51.

Barthel, Michael, Katerina Eva Matsa, and Kirsten Worden. "Coronavirus-Driven Downturn Hits Newspapers Hard as TV News Thrives." Pew Research Center, October 29, 2020. https://www.pewresearch.org/journalism/2020/10/29/coronavirus-driven-downturn-hitsnewspapers-hard-as-tv-news-thrives/.

Bauer, David. "As a Virologist I'm Shocked My Work Has Been Hijacked by Anti-vaxxers." *The Guardian*, September 7, 2021. https://www.theguardian.com/commentisfree/2021/sep/07/virologist-work-anti-vaxxers-covid.

Baym, Nancy. "The New Shape of Online Community." *First Monday* 12, no. 8 (August 2007). http://firstmonday.org/issues/issue12_8/baym/index.html.

Baym, Nancy. *Personal Connections in the Digital Age*. New York: John Wiley and Sons, 2015.

Baym, Nancy. *Playing to the Crowd*. New York: New York University Press, 2018.

Baym, Nancy, and danah boyd. "Socially Mediated Publicness: An Introduction." *Journal of Broadcasting & Electronic Media* 56, no. 3 (2012): 320–29.

Bebawi, Saba, and Diana Bossio, eds. *Social Media and the Politics of Reportage: The "Arab Spring."* London: Palgrave Macmillan, 2014.

Beckett, Charlie, and Mark Deuze. "On the Role of Emotion in the Future of Journalism." *Social Media + Society* 2, no. 3 (2016). https://doi.org/10.117/2056305116662395.

Bedai, Cristiana. "Taking Time Off to Recover from Trauma or Burnout." International Journalists' Network, January 8, 2021. https://ijnet.org/en/resource/taking-time-recover-trauma-or-burnout.

Bélair-Gagnon, Valérie, Diana Bossio, Avery E. Holton, and Logan Molyneux. "Disconnection: How Measured Separations from Journalistic Norms and Labor Can

Help Sustain Journalism." *Social Media + Society* 8, no. 1 (2022). https://doi.org/ 10.1177/20563051221077217.

Bélair-Gagnon, Valérie, and Avery E. Horton. "Boundary Work, Interloper Media, and Analytics in Newsrooms: An Analysis of the Roles of Web Analytics Companies in News Production." *Digital Journalism* 6, no. 4 (March 2018): 492–508.

Bélair-Gagnon, Valérie, Seth C. Lewis, and Colin Agur. "Failure to Launch: Competing Institutional Logics, Intrapreneurship, and the Case of Chatbots." *Journal of Computer-Mediated Communication* 25, no. 4 (July 2020): 291–306. https://doi.org/ 10.1093/JCMC/ZMAA008.

Bélair-Gagnon, Valérie, Jacob Nelson, and Seth C. Lewis. "Audience Engagement, Reciprocity, and the Pursuit of Community Connectedness in Public Media Journalism." *Journalism Practice* 13, no. 5 (2019): 558–75.

Bentivegna, Sara, and Rita Marchetti. "Journalists at a Crossroads: Are Traditional Norms and Practices Challenged by Twitter?" *Journalism* 19, no. 2 (February 2018): 270–90. https://doi.org/10.1177/1464884917716594.

Berger, Jonah, and Katherine L. Milkman. "What Makes Online Content Viral?" *Journal of Marketing Research* 49, no. 2 (April 2012): 192–205. https://doi.org/10.1509/ jmr.10.0353.

Binns, Amy. "Fair Game? Journalists' Experiences of Online Abuse." *Journal of Applied Journalism & Media Studies* 6, no. 2 (2017): 183–206.

Bo, Li, Sarah Stokowski, Stephen W. Dittmore, and Olan K. M. Scott. "For Better or for Worse: The Impact of Social Media on Chinese Sports Journalists." *Communication & Sport* 5, no. 3 (2017): 311–30.

Boateng, Kodwo Jonas Anson, and Redeemer Buatsi. "Face-to-Face with COVID-19: Experiences of Ghanaian Frontline Journalists Infected with the Virus." In *Health Crises and Median Discourses in Sub-Saharan Africa*, edited by Carol Azungi Dralega and Angella Napakol, 147–62. New York: Springer, 2022.

Bossetta, Michael. "The Digital Architectures of Social Media: Comparing Political Campaigning on Facebook, Twitter, Instagram, and Snapchat in the 2016 U.S. Election." *Journalism & Mass Communication Quarterly* 95, no. 2 (June 2018): 471–96.

Bossio, Diana. "Journalists on Instagram: Presenting Professional Identity and Role on Image-Focused Social Media." *Journalism Practice*, November 23, 2021, 1–17. https:// doi.org/10.1080/17512786.2021.2001359.

Bossio, Diana, and Saba Bebawi. "Mapping the Emergence of Social Media in Everyday Journalistic Practices." *Media International Australia* 161, no. 1 (November 2016): 147–58.

Bossio, Diana, and Avery E. Holton. "Burning Out and Turning Off: Journalists' Disconnection Strategies on Social Media." *Journalism* 22, no. 10 (2021): 2475–92.

Bossio, Diana, and Avery E. Holton. "The Identity Dilemma: Identity Drivers and Social Media Fatigue among Journalists." *Popular Communication* 16, no. 4 (2018): 248–62.

Bossio, Diana, Anthony McCosker, Esther Milne, Daniel Golding, and César Albarrán-Torres. "Social Media Managers as Intermediaries: Negotiating the Personal and

Professional in Organizational Communication." *Communication Research and Practice* 6, no. 2 (2020): 95–110.

Bossio, Diana, and Vittoria Sacco. "Defamation in Unbounded Spaces: Journalism and Social Media." In *The Routledge Handbook of Developments in Digital Journalism Studies*, edited by Scott A. Eldridge and Bob Franklin, 336–47. London: Routledge, 2018.

Bossio, Diana, and Vittoria Sacco. "From 'Selfies' to Breaking Tweets: How Journalists Negotiate Personal and Professional Identity on Social Media." *Journalism Practice* 11, no. 5 (May 2017): 527–43.

boyd, danah m., and Nicole Ellison. "Social Network Sites: Definition, History, and Scholarship." *Journal of Computer-Mediated Communication* 13, no. 1 (October 2007): 210–30.

Breed, Warren. "Social Control in the Newsroom: A Functional Analysis." *Social Forces* 33, no. 4 (May 1955): 326–35. https://doi.org/10.2307/2573002.

Brennan, Bonnie. *Opting Out of Digital Media*. London: Routledge, 2019.

Bridgen, Liz. "Emotional Labour and the Pursuit of the Personal Brand: Public Relations Practitioners' Use of Social Media." *Journal of Media Practice* 12, no. 1 (May 2011): 61–76.

Brouillette, Sarah. "Creative Labor." *Mediations* 24, no. 2 (2009): 140–49.

Bucher, Taina, and Anne Helmond. "The Affordances of Social Media Platforms." In *The SAGE Handbook of Social Media*, edited by Jean Burgess, Thomas Poell, and Alice E. Marwick, 233–53. London: SAGE Publications, 2018.

Burger, Ronelle, Brendan Maughan-Brown, Timothy Köhler, René English, and Michele Tameris. "Increased Openness to Accepting a COVID-19 Vaccine Is a Shot in the Arm for South Africa: Evidence from the NIDS-CRAM Wave 5 Survey." National Income Dynamics Study Coronavirus Rapid Mobile Survey (NIDS-CRAM), 2020. https://cramsurvey.org/reports/.

Burke, Ronald J., and Stig Matthiesen. "Workaholism among Norwegian Journalists: Antecedents and Consequences." *Stress and Health* 20, no. 5 (December 2004): 301–8.

Carpenter, Serena, Duygu Kanver, and Rashad Timmons. "It's about Me: A Study of Journalists' Self-Presentation of Their Visual and Verbal Selves." *Journalism Practice* 11, no. 10 (November 2017): 1246–66. https://doi.org/10.1080/17512786.2016.1245587.

Carlson, Matt. *Journalistic Authority: Legitimating News in the Digital Era*. New York: Columbia University Press, 2017.

Carlson, Matt, and Seth C. Lewis. *Boundaries of Journalism*. London: Routledge, 2015.

Cassidy, Elija. "Social Networking Sites and Participatory Reluctance: A Case Study of Gaydar, User Resistance and Interface Rejection." *New Media & Society* 18, no. 11 (December 2016): 2613–28.

Chadwick, Andrew. *The Hybrid Media System: Politics and Power*. New York: Oxford University Press, 2013.

Chang, Clio. "The Substackerati." *Columbia Journalism Review*, Winter 2020. https://www.cjr.org/special_report/substackerati.php.

Cherubini, Frederica, Nic Newman, and Rasmus Kleis Nielsen. "Changing Newsrooms 2021: Hybrid Working and Improving Diversity Remain Twin Challenges for Publishers." *Reuters Institute for the Study of Journalism* 1 (June 2022). https://reutersinstitute.politics.ox.ac.uk/changing-newsrooms-2021-hybrid-working-and-improving-diversity-remain-twin-challenges-publishers.

Clun, Rachel, Melissa Cunningham, and David Estcourt. "Doctors Warn Over 50s Cancelling Appointments Despite Experts Saying Second Doses Are Safe." *Sydney Morning Herald*, June 17, 2021. https://www.smh.com.au/politics/federal/doctors-warn-over-50s-cancellingappointments-despite-expert-second-doses-are-safe-20210617-p581wy.html.

Cobham, Kerry. "How Journalists Can Take Care of Themselves While Covering Trauma." *Poynter*, May 29, 2019. https://www.poynter.org/reporting-editing/2019/how-journalists-can-take-care-of-themselveswhilecovering-trauma.

Coles, Bryn Alexander, and Melanie West. "Trolling the Trolls: Online Forum Users' Constructions of the Nature and Properties of Trolling." *Computers in Human Behavior* 60 (2016): 233–44.

Collinson, David L. "Identities and Insecurities: Selves at Work." *Organization* 10, no. 3 (August 2003): 527–47.

Coomber, Stephen. *Branding*. Mankato, MN: Capstone Publishing, 2002.

"Creating Global Wellbeing and Mental Health Solutions." *CIC Wellbeing*, 2022. https://www.cicwellbeing.com/.

Creech, Brian. *Journalism Education for the Digital Age: Promises, Perils, and Possibilities*. London: Routledge, 2021.

Creech, Brian, and Andrew L. Mendelson. "Imagining the Journalist of the Future: Technological Visions of Journalism Education and Newswork." *Communication Review* 18, no. 2 (2015): 142–65.

Culliford, Elizabeth. "Facebook to Change Rules on Attacking Public Figures on Its Platforms." *Reuters*, October 14, 2021. https://www.reuters.com/technology/exclusive-facebook-changerules-attacking-public-figures-its-platforms-2021–10–13.

Currie Sivek, Susan. "Social Media under Social Control: Regulating Social Media and the Future of Socialization." *Electronic News*, September 9, 2010, 146–64. https://doi.org/10.1177/1931243110383266.

Dalzell, Stephanie. "Australia Signs Deals to Distribute Tens of Millions of Coronavirus Vaccine Doses around the Country." Australian Broadcasting Corporation, December 24, 2020. https://www.abc.net.au/news/2020-12-24/australia-signs-deals-to-distribute-millions-of-covid-19-vaccine/13011476.

Davis, Katlynne. "Examining the Digital Labor of Mental Health Communication on Social Media." In *SIGDOC '21: Proceedings of the 39th ACM International Conference on Design of Communication*, 401–2. New York: Association for Computing Machinery, 2021.

Dean, Jodi. "Communicative Capitalism: Circulation and the Foreclosure of Politics." *Cultural Politics* 1, no. 1 (2005): 51–74.

Deuze, Mark. "Media Life." *Media, Culture & Society* 33, no. 1 (2011): 137–48.

Deuze, Mark. "Media Life, Journalism, and the Entrepreneurial Society." *Australian Journalism Review* 36 (October 2014): 119–31.

Deuze, Mark. "What Is Journalism? Professional Identity and Ideology of Journalists Reconsidered." *Journalism* 6, no. 4 (November 2005): 442–64.

Deuze, Mark. "What Journalism Is (Not)." *Social Media + Society* 5, no. 3 (April 2019). https://doi.org/10.1177/2056305119857202.

Deuze, Mark, and Tamara Witschge. *Beyond Journalism*. New York: John Wiley & Sons, 2020.

Dijck, José Van, Thomas Poell, and Martijn De Waal. *The Platform Society: Public Values in a Connective World*. Oxford: Oxford University Press, 2018.

Djerf-Pierre, Monika, Marina Ghersetti, and Ulrika Hedman. "Appropriating Social Media: The Changing Uses of Social Media among Journalists across Time." *Digital Journalism* 4, no. 7 (March 2016): 849–60.

Djinis, Elizabeth. "Why Are Journalists Leaving Their Full-Time Media Jobs to Go Freelance." *Poynter*, October 6, 2021. https://www.poynter.org/business-work/2021/why-journalists-areleaving-their-full-time-media-jobs-to-go-freelance.

Docherty, Niall. "Facebook's Ideal User: Healthy Habits, Social Capital, and the Politics of Well-Being Online." *Social Media + Society* 6, no. 2 (2020). https://doi.org/10.1177/2056305120915606.

Donsbach, Wolfgang. "Psychology of News Decisions: Factors behind Journalists' Professional Behavior." *Journalism* 5, no. 2 (May 2004): 131–57.

Dubberley, Sam, and Michele Grant. "Journalism and Vicarious Trauma: A Guide for Journalists, Editors and News Organizations." *First Draft*, April 2017. https://firstdraftnews.org/wpcontent/uploads/2017/04/vicarioustrauma.pdf.

Dubberley, Sam, Elizabeth Griffin, and Haluk Mert Bal. "Making Secondary Trauma a Primary Issue: A Study of Eyewitness Media and Vicarious Trauma on the Digital Frontline." Eyewitness Media Hub, November 1, 2015. https://firstdraftnews.org/articles/making-secondary-trauma-primaryissue-study-eyewitness-media-vicarious-trauma-digital-frontline/.

Duffy, Brooke Erin. *(Not) Getting Paid for What You Love*. New Haven, CT: Yale University Press, 2017.

Duffy, Brooke Erin. "The Romance of Work: Gender and Aspirational Labor in the Digital Culture Industries." *International Journal of Cultural Studies* 19, no. 4 (2016): 441–57.

Duffy, Brooke Erin, Annika Pinch, Shruti Sannon, and Megan Sawey. "The Nested Precarities of Creative Labor on Social Media." *Social Media+ Society* 7, no. 2 (2021). https://doi.org/10.1177/20563051211021368.

Fairchild, Charles. "Building the Authentic Celebrity: The 'Idol' Phenomenon in the Attention Economy." *Popular Music and Society* 30, no. 3 (2007): 355–75.

Ferrier, Michelle, and Nisha Garud-Patkar. "TrollBusters: Fighting Online Harassment of Women Journalists." In *Mediating Misogyny: Gender, Technology, and Harassment*, edited by Jacqueline Ryan Vickery and Tracy Everbach, 311–32. New York: Springer International Publishing, 2018.

Ferrucci, Patrick. "Networked: Social Media's Impact on News Production in Digital Newsrooms." *Newspaper Research Journal* 39, no. 1 (2018): 6–17.

"The Field Guide to Security Training in the Newsroom." OpenNews, 2018. https://securitytraining.opennews.org/en/latest/.

Fincham, Kelly. "Business as Usual: How Journalism's Professional Logics Continue to Shape News Organization Policies around Social Media Audiences." *Journalism Practice*, November 2, 2021. https://doi.org/10.1080/17512786.2021.1991437.

Fisher, Caroline. "The Trouble with 'Trust' in News Media." *Communication Research and Practice* 2, no. 4 (2016): 451–65.

Fletcher, Richard, and Rasmus Kleis Nielsen. "Are People Incidentally Exposed to News on Social Media? A Comparative Analysis." *New Media & Society* 20, no. 7 (July 2018): 2450–68.

Foa, Roberto Stefan, and Yascha Mounk. "The Danger of Deconsolidation: The Democratic Disconnect." *Journal of Democracy* 27, no. 3 (2016): 5–17.

Foote, David A., Scott J. Seipel, Nancy B. Johnson, and Michelle K. Duffy. "Employee Commitment and Organizational Policies." *Management Decision* 43, no. 2 (2005): 203–19.

Freelon, Deen, Michael Bossetta, Chris Wells, Josephine Lukito, Yiping Xia, and Kirsten Adams. "Black Trolls Matter: Racial and Ideological Asymmetries in Social Media Disinformation." *Social Science Computer Review* 40, no. 3 (2020). https://journals.sagepub.com/doi/abs/10.1177/0894439320914853.

Gandini, Alessandro. "Digital Work: Self-Branding and Social Capital in the Freelance Knowledge Economy." *Marketing Theory* 16, no. 1 (March 2016): 123–41. https://doi.org/10.1177/1470593115607942.

Gil de Zúñiga, Homero, Brian Weeks, and Alberto Ardèvol-Abreu. "Effects of the News-Finds-Me Perception in Communication: Social Media Use Implications for News Seeking and Learning about Politics." *Journal of Computer-Mediated Communication* 22, no. 3 (2017): 105–23.

Goffman, Erving. *The Presentation of Self in Everyday Life*. Anchor Books. New York: Doubleday, 1959.

González de Bustamante, Celeste, and Jeannine E. Relly. "Journalism in Times of Violence: Social Media Use by US and Mexican Journalists Working in Northern Mexico." *Digital Journalism* 2, no. 4 (2014): 507–23.

Graves, Lucas and Shabbir, Nabeelah. "Gauging the Global impacts of the 'Panama Papers' three years later." (2019). Reuters Institute Factsheet, University of Oxford. https://ora.ox.ac.uk/objects/uuid:6e3081b1–5a91–4ddc-a40b-ad8129591f96/download_file?safe_filename=Graves%2B-%2BGauging%2Bthe%2BGlobal%2BImpacts%2Bof%2Bthe%2BPanama%2BPapers%2BFINAL.pdf&file_format=application%2Fpdf&type_of_work=Report.

Gregg, Melissa. *Counterproductive: Time Management in the Knowledge Economy*. Durham, NC: Duke University Press, 2018.

Gregg, Melissa. *Work's Intimacy*. New York: John Wiley and Sons, 2013.

Grieco, Elizabeth. "Fast Facts about the Newspaper Industry's Financial Struggles as Mc-Clatchy Files for Bankruptcy." Pew Research Center, February 14, 2020. https://www.pewresearch.org/facttank/2020/02/14/fast-facts-about-the-newspaper-industrys-financial-struggles/.

Grieco, Elizabeth. "US Newspapers Have Shed Half of Their Newsroom Employees Since 2008." Pew Research Center, April 20, 2020. https://www.editorandpublisher.com/stories/usnewspapers-have-shed-half-of-their-newsroom-employees-since-2008.

Grover, Steven L. "Fair Workplace Regulation of Internet Usage." *Asia Pacific Management Review* 19, no. 1 (March 2014): 99–115.

Gubana, Benjamin, and Nicolas Perpitch. "WA Health Authorities Report Woman's Death in Hospital, Vaccine History Sent to TGA." Australian Broadcasting Corporation, June 24, 2021. https://www.abc.net.au/news/2021–06–24/woman-death-reported-in-wa-hospital-vaccine-history-probed/100242358.

Hand, Martin. "Visuality in Social Media: Researching Images, Circulations and Practices." In *The SAGE Handbook of Social Media Research Methods*, edited by Anabel Quan-Haase and Luke Sloan, 217–31. London: SAGE, 2022.

Hanusch, Folker, and Axel Bruns. "Journalistic Branding on Twitter: A Representative Study of Australian Journalists' Profile Descriptions." *Digital Journalism* 5, no. 1 (2017): 26–43.

Hargittai, Eszter. "Whose Space? Differences among Users and Non-users of Social Network Sites." *Journal of Computer-Mediated Communication* 13, no. 1 (October 2007): 276–97.

Harlow, Summer. "Protecting News Companies and Their Readers: Exploring Social Media Policies in Latin American Newsrooms." *Digital Journalism* 9, no. 2 (February 2021): 176–95.

Harrison, Teresa, and Brea Barthel. "Wielding New Media in Web 2.0: Exploring the History of Engagement with the Collaborative Construction of Media Products." *New Media & Society* 11, no. 1–2 (2009): 155–78.

Harvey, Adam, Sashka Koloff, and Nick Wiggins. "How Australia's COVID Vaccine Rollout Has Fallen Short and Left Us 'in a Precarious Position.'" *Four Corners*, May 24, 2021. https://www.abc.net.au/news/2021–05–24/australia-covid-vaccine-rollout-what-wentwrong/100151396.

Hayes, Arthur S., Jane B. Singer, and Jerry Ceppos. "Shifting Roles, Enduring Values: The Credible Journalist in a Digital Age." *Journal of Mass Media Ethics* 22, no. 4 (2007): 262–79.

Hedman, Ulrika. "J-Tweeters: Pointing towards a New Set of Professional Practices and Norms in Journalism." *Digital Journalism* 3, no. 2 (April 2014): 279–97.

Hedman, Ulrika. "Making the Most of Twitter: How Technological Affordances Influence Swedish Journalists' Self-Branding." *Journalism* 21, no. 5 (2020): 670–87. https://doi.org/10.1177/2056305115624528.

Hedman, Ulrika, and Monika Djerf-Pierre. "The Social Journalist: Embracing the Social Media Life or Creating a New Digital Divide?" *Digital Journalism* 1, no. 3 (March 2013): 368–85.

Henrichsen, Jennifer R. "Understanding Nascent Newsroom Security and Safety Cultures: The Emergence of the 'Security Champion.'" *Journalism Practice* 16, no. 9 (2021): 1–20.

Herald Sun. "Today's Front Page." Twitter, June 18, 2021. https://twitter.com/theherald sun/status/1405631345699684356.

Hermida, Alfred. "Post-publication Gatekeeping: The Interplay of Publics, Platforms, Paraphernalia, and Practices in the Circulation of News." *Journalism & Mass Communication Quarterly* 97, no. 2 (2020): 469–91.

Hermida, Alfred. "Tweets and Truth: Journalism as a Discipline of Collaborative Verification." *Journalism Practice* 6, no. 5–6 (2012): 659–68.

Hermida, Alfred. "Twitter as an Ambient News Network." In *Twitter and Society*, edited by Katrin Weller, Axel Bruns, Jean Burgess, Merja Mahrt, and Cornelius Puschmann, 359–72. New York: Peter Lang, 2014.

Hermida, Alfred, Seth C. Lewis, and Rodrigo Zamith. "Sourcing the Arab Spring: A Case Study of Andy Carvin's Sources on Twitter during the Tunisian and Egyptian Revolutions." *Journal of Computer-Mediated Communication* 19, no. 3 (2014): 479–99.

Hiltunen, Ilmari. "Trouble in Paradise? Self-Censorship, Outside Interference and Harassment of Journalists in Finland." *Media Asia* 44, no. 1 (2017): 66–70.

Hirst, Martin, and Greg Treadwell. "Blogs Bother Me." *Journalism Practice* 5, no. 4 (February 2011): 446–61.

Hobbs, Allegra. "Substack and the Newsletter Boom: Platform Become a Publisher?" *SAGE Business Cases*, 2021. http://dx.doi.org/10.4135/9781529779349.

Holton, Avery E., Valérie Bélair-Gagnon, Diana Bossio, and Logan Molyneux. "'Not Their Fault, but Their Problem': Organizational Responses to the Online Harassment of Journalists." *Journalism Practice*, July 5, 2021, 1–16. https://doi.org/10.1080/17512786.2021.1946417.

Holton, Avery E., Valérie Bélair-Gagnon, and Cindy Royal. "The Human Side of (News) Engagement Emotion, Platform and Individual Agency." *Digital Journalism* 9, no. 8 (2021): 1184–89. https://doi.org/10.1080/21670811.2021.1930086.

Holton, Avery E., and Seth C. Lewis. "Journalists, Social Media, and the Use of Humor on Twitter." *Electronic Journal of Communication* 21, no. 1–2 (2011). https://d1wqtxts1xzle7.cloudfront.net/6963116/Journalists__social_media__and_the_use_of_humor_on_Twitter-libre.pdf.

Holton, Avery E., and Logan Molyneux. "Identity Lost? The Personal Impact of Brand Journalism." *Journalism: Theory, Practice & Criticism* 18, no. 2 (February 2017): 195–210. https://doi.org/10.1177/1464884915608816.

"Identifying and Tackling Manipulated Media." Reuters, 2022. https://www.reuters.com/manipulatedmedia.

"Impact of COVID19 on East African Women Journalists." African Women in Media (AWiM). https://africanwomeninmedia.com/impact-covid19-east-african -women-journalists/.

"Infodemic." World Health Organisation. Last modified November 29, 2022. https:// www.who.int/health-topics/infodemic#tab=tab_1.

Ingram, Matthew. "Social Media Crackdowns at the Times and Journal Will Backfire." *Columbia Journalism Review*, October 20, 2017. https://www.cjr.org/criticism/social -media-twitter-times-journal.php.

"IPI Launches New Video Tutorials on Online Harassment." International Press Institute, January 27, 2020. https://ipi.media/ipi-launches-new-video-tutorials-on -online-harassment/.

Jamil, Sadia. "Suffering in Silence: The Resilience of Pakistan's Female Journalists to Combat Sexual Harassment, Threats and Discrimination." *Journalism Practice* 14, no. 2 (2020): 150–170.

Jamiu, Abiodun. "This Organization in Nigeria Caters to Journalists' Mental Health." International Journalists' Network, March 18, 2022. https://ijnet.org/en/story/ organization-nigeria-catersjournalists-mental-health/.

Jenkins, Henry. *Convergence Culture: Where Old and New Media Collide*. Cambridge, MA: MIT Press, 2008.

Jeong, Sarah. "Casey Newton on Leaving 'The Verge' for Substack and the Future of Tech Journalism." *Medium*, September 23, 2020. https://onezero.medium.com/casey -newton-on-leaving-the-verge for-substack-and-the-future-of-tech-journalism -974a646375fa.

Jian, Guowei, and Ting Liu. "Journalist Social Media Practice in China: A Review and Synthesis." *Journalism* 19, no. 9–10 (September 2018): 1452–70. https://doi.org/ 10.1177/1464884918778257.

Jones, Tom. "NBC News Defends a Reporter after a Bizarre Tucker Carlson Criticism." *Poynter*, October 20, 2020. https://www.poynter.org/ethics-trust/2020/nbc-news -defends-a-reporter-after-a-bizarre-tucker-carlson-criticism/.

"Journalism Essentials." American Press Institute. Last modified June 1, 2022. https:// www.americanpressinstitute.org/journalism-essentials/what-isjournalism/ #:~:text=Journalism%20is%20the%20activity%20of,certain%20identifiable%20 charcteristics%20and%20practices.

"Journalists' Mental Health during the Pandemic: We Need to Talk." International Federation of Journalists. Last modified April 21, 2021. https://www.ifj.org/mediacentre/ news/detail/category/press-releases/article/journalists-mental-health-during -the-pandemic-we-need-to-talk.html.

Jukes, Stephen, Karen Fowler-Watt, and Gavin Rees. "Reporting the Covid-19 Pandemic: Trauma on Our Own Doorstep." *Digital Journalism* 10, no. 6 (2021): 1–18.

Jung, Jaemin, and Youngju Kim. "Causes of Newspaper Firm Employee Burnout in Korea and Its Impact on Organizational Commitment and Turnover Intention." *International Journal of Human Resource Management* 23, no. 17 (February 2012): 3636–51.

Kalleberg, Arne L. "Precarious Work, Insecure Workers: Employment Relations in Transition." *American Sociological Review* 74, no. 1 (2009): 1–22.

Kane, Gerald C., Robert G. Fichman, John Gallaugher, and John Glaser. "Community Relations 2.0." *Harvard Business Review* 87, no. 11 (2009): 45–50.

Kania-Lundholm, Magdalena. "Why Disconnecting Matters? Towards a Critical Research Agenda on Online Disconnection." In *Reckoning with Social Media: Disconnection in the Age of the Techlash*, edited by Aleena Chia, Ana Jorge, and Tero Karppi, 13–37. Lanham, MD: Rowman and Littlefield, 2021.

Karlsson, Michael. "Dispersing the Opacity of Transparency in Journalism on the Appeal of Different Forms of Transparency to the General Public." *Journalism Studies* 21, no. 13 (2020): 1795–1814.

Karppi, Tero. "Digital Suicide and the Biopolitics of Leaving Facebook." *Transformations* 20 (2011): 1–28.

Karppi, Tero. *Disconnect: Facebook's Affective Bonds*. Minneapolis: University of Minnesota Press, 2018.

Karppi, Tero. "Disconnect Me: User Engagement and Facebook." PhD diss., University of Turku, 2014.

Karppi, Tero, Aleena Chia, Airi Lampinen, Zeena Feldman, Michael Dieter, Pedro Ferreira, and Alex Beattie. "Disconnection: Designs and Desires." AoIR Selected Papers of Internet Research, 2020. https://spir.aoir.org/ojs/index.php/spir/article/view/11130.

Kefi, Hajer, and Daniel Maar. "The Power of Lurking: Assessing the Online Experience of Luxury Brand Fan Page Followers." *Journal of Business Research* 117 (2020): 579–86.

Kirpal, Simone, and Alan Brown. "The Much Vaunted 'Flexible Employee'-What Does It Take?" In *Identities at Work*, edited by Alan Brown, Simone Kirpal, and Felix Rauner, 211–38. Dordrecht: Springer, 2007.

Klaas, Brian S., and Hoyt N. Wheeler. "Managerial Decision Making about Employee Discipline: A Policy-Capturing Approach." *Personnel Psychology* 43, no. 1 (March 1990): 117–34.

Klawitter, Erin, and Eszter Hargittai. "'It's Like Learning a Whole Other Language': The Role of Algorithmic Skills in the Curation of Creative Goods." *International Journal of Communication* 12 (2018): 3490–3510.

Koirala, Samiksha. "Female Journalists' Experience of Online Harassment: A Case Study of Nepal." *Media and Communication* 8, no. 1 (2020): 47–56.

Kovach, Bill, and Tom Rosenstiel. *The Elements of Journalism: What Newspeople Should Know and the Public Should Expect*. New York: Three Rivers Press, 2007.

La, Viet-Phuong, Thanh-Hang Pham, Manh-Toan Ho, Minh-Hoang Nguyen, Khanh-Linh P. Nguyen, Thu-Trang Vuong, and Hong-Kong T. Nguyen. "Policy Response, Social Media and Science Journalism for the Sustainability of the Public Health System amid the COVID-19 Outbreak: The Vietnam Lessons." *Sustainability* 12, no. 7 (2020): 2931.

Lasén, Amparo. "Digital Self-Portraits, Exposure and the Modulation of Intimacy." in *Mobile and Digital Communication*, edited by Jose R. Carvalheiro and Ana S. Tellería, 61–68. Covillã: LabCom, 2015.

Lasén, Amparo, and Edgar Gómez-Cruz. "Digital Photography and Picture Sharing: Redefining the Public/Private Divide." *Knowledge, Technology & Policy* 22, no. 3 (September 2009): 205–15. https://link.springer.com/article/10.1007/s12130-009-9086-8.

Lasorsa, Dominic L., Seth C. Lewis, and Avery Horton. "Normalizing Twitter." *Journalism Studies* 13, no. 1 (April 2011): 19–36.

Leaver, Tama, Tim Highfield, and Crystal Abidin. *Instagram: Visual Social Media Cultures*. New York: John Wiley and Sons, 2020.

Lee, Jayeon. "The Double-Edged Sword: The Effects of Journalists' Social Media Activities on Audience Perceptions of Journalists and Their News Products." *Journal of Computer-Mediated Communication* 20, no. 3 (May 2015): 312–29. https://doi.org/10.1111/jcc4.12113.

Lee, Jayeon. "'Friending' Journalists on Social Media: Effects on Perceived Objectivity and Intention to Consume News." *Journalism Studies* 21, no. 15 (November 2020): 2096–2112. https://doi.org/10.1080/1461670X.2020.1810102.

Lee, Jayeon. "Opportunity or Risk? How News Organizations Frame Social Media in Their Guidelines for Journalists." *Communication Review* 19, no. 2 (April 2016): 106–27.

Lemke, Jeslyn. "Pushing a Political Agenda: Harassment of French and African Journalists in Côte d'Ivoire's 2010–2011 National Election Crisis." *International Journal of Communication* 14 (2020): 472–90.

Lewis, Seth. "Reciprocity as a Key Concept for Social Media and Society." *Social Media + Society* 1, no. 1 (2015). https://journals.sagepub.com/doi/full/10.1177/2056305115580339.

Lewis, Seth C., and Logan Molyneux. "A Decade of Research on Social Media and Journalism: Assumptions, Blind Spots, and a Way Forward." *Media and Communication* 6, no. 4 (November 2018): 11–23.

Libert, Manon, Florence Le Cam, and David Domingo. "Belgian Journalists in Lockdown: Survey on Employment and Working Conditions and Representations of Their Role." *Journalism Studies* 23, no. 5–6 (2022): 588–610.

Light, Ben. *Disconnecting with Social Networking Sites*. Basingstoke: Palgrave Macmillan, 2014.

Light, Ben, and Elija Cassidy. "Strategies for the Suspension and Prevention of Connection: Rendering Disconnection as Socioeconomic Lubricant with Facebook." *New Media & Society* 16, no. 7 (November 2014): 1169–84.

Liu, Dong, Sarah E. Ainsworth, and Roy F. Baumeister. "A Meta-analysis of Social Networking Online and Social Capital." *Review of General Psychology* 20, no. 4 (December 2016): 369–91.

Livingston, Steven, and Gregory Asmolov. "Networks and the Future of Foreign Affairs Reporting." *Journalism Studies* 11, no. 5 (September 2010): 745–60.

Livingstone, Sonia. *Audiences and Publics: When Cultural Engagement Matters for the Public Sphere*. Bristol: Intellect, 2005.

Lopez, Kimberly J., Meghan L. Muldoon, and Janet K. L. McKeown. "One Day of #Feminism: Twitter as a Complex Digital Arena for Wielding, Shielding, and Trolling Talk on Feminism." *Leisure Sciences* 41, no. 3 (2019): 203–20.

Lough, Kyser, Logan Molyneux, and Avery E. Holton. "A Clearer Picture: Journalistic Identity in Words and Images on Twitter." *Journalism Practice* 12, no. 10 (November 2018): 1277–91. https://doi.org/10.1080/17512786.2017.1389292.

Lowery, Wilson. "Journalism Innovation and the Ecology of News Production: Institutional Tendencies." *Journalism & Communication Monographs* 14, no. 4 (December 2012): 214–87.

Lutz, Christoph, and Christian Pieter Hoffman. "The Dark Side of Online Participation: Exploring Non-, Passive and Negative Participation." *Information, Communication & Society* 20, no. 6 (2017): 876–97.

Maares, Phoebe, and Folker Hanusch. "Exploring the Boundaries of Journalism: Instagram Micro Bloggers in the Twilight Zone of Lifestyle Journalism." *Journalism* 21, no. 2 (2020): 262–78.

MacDonald, Jasmine B., Anthony J. Saliba, Gene Hodgins, and Linda A. Ovington. "Burnout in Journalists: A Systematic Literature Review." *Burnout Research* 3, no. 2 (June 2016): 34–44.

Mahone, Jessica, Qun Wang, Phillip Napoli, Matthew Weber, and Katie McCollough. "Who's Producing Local Journalism? Assessing Journalistic Output across Different Outlet Types." DeWitt Wallace Center for Media & Democracy Report, August 2019. https://www.researchgate.net/publication/335455265_Who's_Producing _Local_JournalismAssessing_Journalistic_Output_Across_Different_Outlet _Types.

Martin, Fiona. "Tackling Gendered Violence Online: Evaluating Digital Safety Strategies for Women Journalists." *Australian Journalism Review* 20, no. 2 (2018): 73–89.

Martin, Fiona, and Colleen Murrell. "Negotiating the Conversation: How Journalists Learn to Interact with Audiences Online." *Journalism Practice* 15, no. 6 (2021): 839–59.

Maruca, Julia. "Post-Gazette Staffers Are Posting Tweet That Got a Black Reporter Removed from Protest Coverage in Solidarity." *Pittsburgh City Paper*, June 5, 2020. https:// www.pghcitypaper.com/pittsburgh/post-gazette-staffers-are-posting-tweet -that-got-a black-reporter-removed-from-protest-coverage-in-solidarity/Content ?oid=17409693.

Marwick, Alice. "Instafame: Luxury Selfies in the Attention Economy." *Public Culture* 27, no. 1 (2015): 137–60.

Marwick, Alice. *Status Update: Celebrity, Publicity, and Branding in the Social Media Age*. New Haven, CT: Yale University Press, 2013.

Marwick, Alice E., and danah boyd. "I Tweet Honestly, I Tweet Passionately: Twitter Users, Context Collapse, and the Imagined Audience." *New Media & Society* 13, no. 1 (February 2011): 14–33. https://doi.org/10.1177/1461444810365313.

Marwick, Alice E., and danah boyd. "Networked Privacy: How Teenagers Negotiate Context in Social Media." *New Media & Society* 16, no. 7 (November 2014): 1051–67. https://doi.org/10.1177/1461444814543995.

Maslach, Christina, and Susan Jackson. "The Measurement of Experienced Burnout." *Journal of Occupational Behavior* 2, no. 99 (April 1981): 99–113.

Masullo Chen, Gina, Paromita Pain, Victoria Y. Chen, Madlin Mekelburg, Nina Springer, and Franziska Troger. "'You Really Have to Have a Thick Skin': A Cross-Cultural Perspective on How Online Harassment Influences Female Journalists." *Journalism* 21, no. 7 (2020): 877–95.

Mathews, Nick, Valérie Bélair-Gagnon, and Matt Carlson. "'Why I Quit Journalism': Former Journalists' Advice Giving as a Way to Regain Control." *Journalism* 24, no. 1 (January 2023): 62–77. https://doi.org/10.1177/14648849211061958.

Mattar, Pacinthe. "Objectivity Is a Privilege Afforded to White Journalists." *The Walrus*. Last updated February 10, 2022. https://thewalrus.ca/objectivity-is-a-privilege -afforded-to-white journalists/.

McCosker, Anthony, and Amelia Johns. "Contested Publics: Racist Rants, Bystander Action and Social Media Acts of Citizenship." *Media International Australia* 151, no. 1 (2014): 66–72.

McMahon, Neil. "Five Welcome Voices Guiding Victorians through COVID." *The Age*, September 5, 2021. https://www.theage.com.au/national/victoria/five-welcome -voices-guiding-victoriansthrough-covid-20210903-p58ohw.html.

Mellado, Claudia, Lea Hellmueller, and Wolfgang Donsbach. *Journalistic Role Performance: Concepts, Contexts, and Methods*. New York: Routledge, 2016.

Mellado, Claudia, Lea Hellmueller, Mireya Márquez-Ramírez, Maria Luisa Humanes, Colin Sparks, Agnieszka Stepinska, Svetlana Pasti, Anna-Maria Schielicke, Edson Tandoc, and Haiyan Wang. "The Hybridization of Journalistic Cultures: A Comparative Study of Journalistic Role Performance." *Journal of Communication* 67, no. 6 (2017): 944–67.

Mellado, Claudia, and Alfred Hermida. "A Conceptual Framework for Journalistic Identity on Social Media: How the Personal and Professional Contribute to Power and Profit." *Digital Journalism*, May 5, 2021, 1–16. https://doi.org/10.1080/21670811 .2021.1907203.

Mellado, Claudia, and Auska Ovando. "How Chilean Journalists Use Social Media: Digital Transformation and New Forms of Visibility and Identity Creation." *Palabra Clave* 24, no. 2 (2021): 1–26.

Menezes, Neia Prata, Muloongo Simuzingili, Zelalem Yilma Debebe, Fedja Pivodic, and Ernest Massiah. "What Is Driving COVID-19 Vaccine Hesitancy in Sub-Saharan Africa?" *World Bank Blogs*, 2021. https://blogs.worldbank.org/africacan/what-driving -covid-19-vaccine-hesitancysub-saharan-africa.

Messing, Solomon, and Sean J. Westwood. "Selective Exposure in the Age of Social Media: Endorsements Trump Partisan Source Affiliation When Selecting News Online." *Communication Research* 41, no. 8 (2014): 1042–63.

"Meta Investor Relations." Meta. Last modified November 29, 2022. https://investor
.fb.com/resources/default.aspx.

Mihailidis, Paul, and Samantha Viotty. "Spreadable Spectacle in Digital Culture: Civic
Expression, Fake News, and the Role of Media Literacies in 'Post-Fact' Society."
American Behavioral Scientist 61, no. 4 (2017): 441–54.

Mioli, Theresa. "Mental Health and Wellbeing of Journalists Take Center Stage for
Panel Discussion at ISOJ." ISOJ, February 28, 2022. https://isoj.org/mental-health
-and-wellbeing-of-journaliststake-center-stage-for-panel-discussion-at-isoj/.

Mitchell, Amy, and Jacob Liedke. "About Four in Ten Americans Say Social Media Is an
Important Way of Following COVID-19 Vaccine News." Pew Research Center, August 24, 2021. https://www.pewresearch.org/fact-tank/2021/08/24/about-four-in
-ten-americans-say-social media-is-an-important-way-of-following-covid-19
-vaccine-news.

Mitra, Tanushree, Scott Counts, and James W. Pennebaker. "Understanding Antivaccination Attitudes in Social Media." In *Tenth International AAAI Conference on Web
and Social Media*, 2016. https://ojs.aaai.org/index.php/ICWSM/article/view/14729.

Molyneux, Logan. "A Personalized Self-Image: Gender and Branding Practices among
Journalists." *Social Media + Society* 5, no. 3 (July 2019). https://doi.org/10.1177/
2056305119872950.

Molyneux, Logan. "What Journalists Retweet: Opinion, Humor, and Brand Development on Twitter." *Journalism: Theory, Practice & Criticism* 16, no. 7 (October 2015):
920–35. https://doi.org/10.1177/1464884914550135.

Molyneux, Logan, and Avery Holton. "Branding (Health) Journalism: Perceptions,
Practices, and Emerging Norms." *Digital Journalism* 3, no. 2 (March 2015): 225–42.
https://doi.org/10.1080/21670811.2014.906927.

Molyneux, Logan, Avery Holton, and Seth C. Lewis. "How Journalists Engage in
Branding on Twitter: Individual, Organizational, and Institutional Levels." *Information, Communication & Society* 21, no. 10 (2018): 1386–1401.

Molyneux, Logan, Seth C. Lewis, and Avery E. Holton. "Media Work, Identity, and
the Motivations That Shape Branding Practices among Journalists: An Explanatory
Framework." *New Media & Society* 21, no. 4 (2019): 836–55.

Molyneux, Logan, and Rachel R. Mourão. "Political Journalists' Normalization of
Twitter: Interaction and New Affordances." *Journalism Studies* 20, no. 2 (October
2017): 1–19.

Mossberger, Karen, Caroline J. Tolbert, and Ramona S. McNeal. *Digital Citizenship: The
Internet, Society, and Participation*. Cambridge, MA: MIT Press, 2007.

Mourão, Rachel R., and Logan Molyneux. "Tweeting outside the Lines: Normalization
and Fragmentation as Political Reporters Break from the Mainstream." *Journalism
Practice*, May 31, 2020, 1–19. https://doi.org/10.1080/17512786.2020.1771753.

Mourão, Rachel R., and Craig T. Robertson. "Fake News as Discursive Integration: An
Analysis of Sites That Publish False, Misleading, Hyperpartisan and Sensational
Information." *Journalism Studies* 20, no. 14 (2019): 2077–95.

Murphy, John M. *Branding: A Key Marketing Tool*. Princeton, NJ: McGraw-Hill Companies, 1987.

Nel, Francois, and Oscar Westlund. "The 4C's of Mobile News: Channels, Conversation, Content and Commerce." *Journalism Practice* 6, no. 5–6 (March 2012): 744–53.

Nelson, Jacob L., and Seth C. Lewis. "Only 'Sheep' Trust Journalists? How Citizens' Self Perceptions Shape Their Approach to News." *New Media & Society*, 2021. https://journals.sagepub.com/doi/full/10.1177/14614448211018160.

Newman, Nic, Richard Fletcher, Anne Schulz, Simge Andı, Craig T. Robertson, and Rasmus Kleis Nielsen. "Digital News Report 2021." Reuters Institute for the Study of Journalism, 2021. https://reutersinstitute.politics.ox.ac.uk/digital-news-report/2021.

Newport, Cal. *Digital Minimalism*. Camberwell, VIC: Penguin Press, 2019.

Nkie Mongo, Cleves. "The Practice of Envelope Journalism in the Republic of the Congo." *Newspaper Research Journal* 42, no. 1 (February 2021): 111–26. https://doi.org/10.1177/0739532921990763.

Opgenhaffen, Michaël, and Harald Scheerlinck. "Social Media Guidelines for Journalists: An Investigation into the Sense and Nonsense among Flemish Journalists." *Journalism Practice* 8, no. 6 (November 2014): 726–41.

Orlowski, Jeff, dir. 2020. *The Social Dilemma*. Netflix, Video on Demand.

Örnebring, Henrik. "Journalists Thinking about Precarity: Making Sense of the 'New Normal.'" In *International Symposium on Online Journalism* 8 (2018): 109–27.

Papacharissi, Zizi. *Affective Publics: Sentiment, Technology, and Politics*. Oxford: Oxford University Press, 2015.

Papacharissi, Zizi. "Without You, I'm Nothing: Performances of the Self on Twitter." *International Journal of Communication* 6 (2012): 1989–2006.

Papadakis, Maria. *Computer-Mediated Communities: The Implications of Information, Communication, and Computational Technologies for Creating Community Online*. Arlington: SRI International, 2003.

Park, Chang Sup, and Barbara K. Kaye. "What's This? Incidental Exposure to News on Social Media, News-Finds-Me Perception, News Efficacy, and News Consumption." *Mass Communication and Society* 23, no. 2 (2020): 157–80.

Park, Sora, Caroline Fisher, Kieran McGuinness, Jee Young Lee, and Kerry McCallum. "Digital News Report: Australia 2021." News and Media Research Centre, University of Canberra, 2021. https://www.canberra.edu.au/research/faculty-research-centres/nmrc/digital-news-reportaustralia-2021.

Patel, Sahil. "'A Fun Adventure, Not a Business': The Weather Channel Stopped Publishing Video on Facebook." *Digiday*, May 23, 2018. https://digiday.com/media/the-weather-channel-has walked-away-from-facebook-video.

Paulussen, Steve. "Technology and the Transformation of News Work: Are Labor Conditions in (Online) Journalism Changing." In *The Handbook of Global Online Journalism*, edited by Eugenia Siapera and Andreas Veglis, 192–208. New York: John Wiley and Sons, 2012.

Pearson, Luke. "Nothing about Us, without Us. That's Why We Need Indigenous-Owned Media." *The Guardian Australia*, August 3, 2015. https://www.theguardian.com/

commentisfree/2015/aug/03/nothing-about-us-without-us-thats-why-we-need
-indigenous-owned-media.

Pelaprat, Etienne, and Barry Brown. "Reciprocity: Understanding Online Social Relations." *First Monday* 17, no. 10 (October 2012). https://journals.uic.edu/ojs/index
.php/fm/article/download/3324/3330.

Perreault, Gregory, and Valerie Bélair-Gagnon. "The Lifestyle of Lifestyle Journalists."
Journalism Practice, August 11, 2022. https://doi.org/10.1080/17512786.2022.2111697.

Perreault, Mildred F., and Gregory P. Perreault. "Journalists on COVID-19 Journalism:
Communication Ecology of Pandemic Reporting." *American Behavioral Scientist* 65,
no. 7 (June 2021): 976–91.

Peters, Jonathan. "Lawsuits over Journalist Twitter Accounts May Become More
Common." *Columbia Journalism Review*, September 10, 2018. https://www.cjr.org/
united_states_project/roanoke-times-twitter.php.

Peters, Tom. "The Brand Called You." *Fast Company* 10, no. 10 (1997): 83–87.

Philips, Whitney. *This Is Why We Can't Have Nice Things: Mapping the Relationship between
Online Trolling and Mainstream Culture.* Cambridge, MA: MIT Press, 2015.

Pickard, Victor. "The Misinformation Society." In *Antidemocracy in America: Truth, Power
and the Republic at Risk*, edited by Eric Klinenberg, Caitlin Zaloom, and Sharon Mar-
cus, 39–48. New York: Columbia University Press, 2019.

Pindayi, Brian. "Social Media Uses and Effects: The Case of Whatsapp in Africa." In
Impacts of the Media on African Socio-economic Development, edited by Okorie Nes-
lon, Babatunde Raphael Ojebuyi, and Abiodun Salawu, 34–51. Hershey, PA: IGI
Global, 2017.

"Policies and Standards." *Washington Post*, January 1, 2021. https://www.washington
post.com/policies-and-standards/.

Portwood-Stacer, Laura. "Media Refusal and Conspicuous Non-consumption: The
Performative and Political Dimensions of Facebook Abstention." *New Media &
Society* 15, no. 7 (2013): 1041–57.

Posetti, Julie. "Combating Online Abuse: When Journalists and Their Sources Are Targeted." In *Journalism, "Fake News" and Disinformation: A Handbook for Journalism Education
and Training*, ed. Cherilyn Ireton and Julie Posetti, 109–19. Paris: UNESCO, 2018.

Posetti, Julie. "Fighting Back against Online Harassment: Maria Ressa." In *An Attack
on One Is an Attack on All: Successful Initiatives to Protect Journalists and Combat Impunity*,
edited by Larry Kilman, 37–40. Paris: UNESCO, 2017.

Posetti, Julie. "The New Frontline." In *Insight from Peace Reporting*, edited by Kristin
Skare Orgeret. New York: Routledge, 2021.

Posetti, Julie, Emily Bell, and Pete Brown. *Journalism and the Pandemic: A Global Snapshot
of Impacts.* International Center for Journalists (ICFJ) and Tow Center for Digital
Journalism, 2020. https://www.icfj.org/sites/default/files/202010/Journalism%20
and%20the%20Pandemic%20Project%20Report%201%202020_FINAL.df.

Posetti, Julie, Nabeelah Shabbir, Diana Maynard, Kalina Bontcheva, and Nermine
Aboulez. *The Chilling: Global Trends in Online Violence against Women Journalists.*
UNESCO, 2021. https://unesdoc.unesco.org/ark:/48223/pf0000377223.

Powers, Matthew, and Sandra Vera-Zambrano. "How Journalists Use Social Media in France and the United States: Analyzing Technology Use across Journalistic Fields." *New Media & Society* 20, no. 8 (August 2018): 2728–44.

Prassl, Jeremias. *Humans as a Service: The Promise and Perils of Work in the Gig Economy*. Oxford: Oxford University Press, 2018.

Prata Menezes, Neia, Muloongo Simuzingili, Zelalem Yilma Debebe, Fedja Pivodic, and Ernest Massiah. "What Is Driving COVID-19 Vaccine Hesitancy in Sub-Saharan Africa?" *World Bank Blogs*, August 11, 2021. https://blogs.worldbank.org/africacan/what-driving-covid-19-vaccinehesitancy-sub-saharan-africa.

Prior, Markus. "News vs. Entertainment: How Increasing Media Choice Widens Gaps in Political Knowledge and Turnout." *Political Science* 49, no. 3 (2005): 577–92.

"Promoting the Physical and Emotional Safety of Journalists in Canada and Abroad." Canadian Journalism Forum on Violence and Trauma, 2020. https://sites.google.com/a/journalismforum.ca/main-forum-site/home.

Qiu, Jack L., Melissa Gregg, and Kate Crawford. "Circuits of Labor: A Labor Theory of the iPhone Era." *TripleC: Communication, Capitalism & Critique* 12, no. 2 (September 2014): 564–81.

Raun, Tobias. "Capitalizing Intimacy: New Subcultural Forms of Micro-celebrity Strategies and Affective Labour on YouTube." *Convergence* 24, no. 1 (2018): 99–113.

Rees, Gavin. "Handling Traumatic Imagery: Developing a Standard Operating Procedure." Dart Center, April 4, 2017. https://dartcenter.org/resources/handling-traumatic-imagery-developingstandard-operating-procedure.

Reese, Stephen D. *The Crisis of the Institutional Press*. New York: John Wiley and Sons, 2020.

Reinardy, Scott. "Newspaper Journalism in Crisis: Burnout on the Rise, Eroding Young Journalists' Career Commitment." *Journalism* 12, no. 1 (2011): 33–50.

"Reporters Exposed to Traumatic Events: Tips for Managers and Editors." Dart Center, February 11, 2013. https://dartcenter.org/content/tips-for-managers-and-editors-news-personnel-exposed-totraumatic-events.

Reuters. "Who Is Nobel Peace Prize Winner Maria Ressa?" *SBS Online*, October 9, 2021. https://www.sbs.com.au/news/who-is-nobel-peace-prize-winner-maria-ressa/80069978-124f4390-b947-8fc31acb073d.

Robertson, Katie. "Reporter Felicia Sonmez Is Fired by the Washington Post." *New York Times*, June 9, 2022. https://www.nytimes.com/2022/06/09/business/media/felicia-sonmez-washingtonpost.html.

Robertson, Katie. "Two Texas Tribune Leaders Announce Their Departures after a Year on the Job." *New York Times*, March 30, 2021. https://www.nytimes.com/2021/03/30/business/media/texas-tribune-ishmael-tran.html.

Robinson, Sue. "'Journalism as Process': The Organizational Implications of Participatory Online News." *Journalism & Communication Monographs* 13, no. 3 (September 2011): 137–210.

Ryfe, David. *Can Journalism Survive? An Inside Look at American Newsrooms*. Cambridge: Polity Books, 2013.

Ryfe, David. "The Ontology of Journalism." *Journalism* 20, no. 1 (December 2018): 206–9.

Sacco, Vittoria, and Diana Bossio. "Don't Tweet This! How Journalists and Media Organizations Negotiate Tensions Emerging from the Implementation of Social Media Policy in Newsrooms." *Digital Journalism* 5, no. 2 (2017): 177–93.

Sales, Leigh. "Bullying on Twitter Has Become Unhinged. It's Time to Call Out the Personal, Sexist Attacks." *ABC News*, September 14, 2021. https://www.abc.net.au/news/2021–09–14/twittersocial-media-bullies-political-journalism/10045871.

Satchell, Christine, and Paul Dourish. "Beyond the User: Use and Non-use of HCI." In *Proceedings OZCHI 9–16, 49th Hawaii International Conference on System Sciences*, 3888–97. Koloa, 2016.

Saunokonoko, Mark. "Not a Race? The Graphs That Rank Australia Dead Last." *Nine News*, June 30, 2021. https://www.9news.com.au/national/coronavirus-australia-dead-last-in-oecd-forvaccinated-people/51dbd565–25fe-4e07-891f-2c689c39c467.

Schiffrin, Anya. "Credibility and Trust in Journalism." In *Oxford Research Encyclopedia of Communication*, edited by J. Naussbaum Oxford: Oxford University Press, 2019. https://doi.org/10.1093/acrefore/9780190228613.013.794.

Schneider, Gabe. "Journalism Outlets Need New Social Media Policies." Reynolds Journalism Institute, 2020. https://rjionline.org/reporting/journalism-outlets-need-new-social-mediapolicies.

Scolere, Leah, Urszula Pruchniewska, and Brooke Erin Duffy. "Constructing the Platform-Specific Self-Brand: The Labor of Social Media Promotion." *Social Media + Society* 4, no. 3 (July 2018). https://doi.org/10.1177/2056305118784768.

Seely, Natalee. "Journalists and Mental Health: The Psychological Toll of Covering Everyday Trauma." *Newspaper Research Journal* 40, no. 2 (2019): 239–59.

Selwyn, Neil. "Digital Division or Digital Decision? A Study of Non-users and Low Users of Computers." *Poetics* 34, no. 4–5 (2006): 273–92.

Senft, Theresa. "Microcelebrity and the Branded Self." *A Companion to New Media Dynamics* 11 (2013): 346–54.

Shearer, Elisa. "Local News Is Playing an Important Role for Americans during CO-VID-19 Outbreak." Pew Research Center, July 2, 2021. https://www.pewresearch.org/facttank/2020/07/02/local-news-is-playing-an-important-role-for-americans-during-covid-19 outbreak/.

Siguru, Wahutu. "Prophets without Honor: Peripheral Actors in Kenyan Journalism." *Media and Communication* 7, no. 4 (2019). https://www.cogitatiopress.com/mediaandcommunication/article/view/2552.

Šimunjak, Maja. "Pride and Anxiety: British Journalists' Emotional Labour in the Covid-19 Pandemic." *Journalism Studies* 23, no. 3 (2022): 320–37.

Singer, Jane B. "The Ethics of Social Journalism." *Australian Journalism Review* 34, no. 1 (2012): 3–16.

Singer, Jane, David Domingo, Ari Heinonen, Alfred Hermida, Steve Paulussen, Thorsten Quandt, Zvi Reich, and Marina Vujnovic. *Participatory Journalism: Guarding Open Gates at Online Newspapers.* New York: Wiley-Blackwell, 2011.

Siraj-Blatchford, Iram. "Educational Research and Reform: Some Implications for the Professional Identity of Early Years Teachers." *British Journal of Educational Studies* 41, no. 4 (1993). https://doi.org/10.1080/00071005.1993.9973975.

Six, Frédérique, and Arndt Sorge. "Creating a High-Trust Organization: An Exploration into Organizational Policies That Stimulate Interpersonal Trust Building." *Journal of Management Studies* 45, no. 5 (July 2008): 857–84.

Smith, Ben. "Survey Says: Never Tweet." *New York Times*, February 1, 2021. https://www.nytimes.com/2021/01/31/business/media/journalists-twitter.html.

"Social Media Guidelines for the Times Newsroom." *New York Times*, October 13, 2017. https://www.nytimes.com/2017/10/13/reader-center/social-media-guidelines.htm.

"Special Section: Social Media." National Public Radio, February 11, 2017. https://www.npr.org/about-npr/688418842/special-section-social-media.

Staender, Anna, Edda Humprecht, Frank Esser, Sophie Morosoli, and Peter Van Aelst. "Is Sensationalist Disinformation More Effective? Three Facilitating Factors at the National, Individual, and Situational Level." *Digital Journalism* 10, no. 6 (2021): 976–96.

Stieglitz, Stefan, and Linh Dang-Xuan. "Emotions and Information Diffusion in Social Media Sentiment of Microblogs and Sharing Behavior." *Journal of Management Information Systems* 29, no. 4 (April 2013): 217–48.

Straub, Caroline, Claartje J. Vinkenburg, Marco van Kleef, and Joeri Hofmans. "Effective HR Implementation: The Impact of Supervisor Support for Policy Use on Employee Perceptions and Attitudes." *International Journal of Human Resource Management* 29, no. 22 (2018): 3115–35.

Strom, Hannah. "It's Time for Newsrooms to Tackle Taboos about Mental Health. Here's How." Reuters Institute for the Study of Journalism, September 11, 2020. https://reutersinstitute.politics.ox.ac.uk/risj-review/its-time-newsrooms-tackle-taboos-about mental-health-heres-how.

Sullivan, Margaret. "Online Harassment of Female Journalists Is Real, and It's Increasingly Hard to Endure." *Washington Post*, March 13, 2021. https://www.washingtonpost.com/lifestyle/media/online-harassmentfemale-journalists/2021/03/13/ed24b0aa-82aa-11eb-ac37-4383f7709abe_story.html.

Syvertsen, Trine. *Digital Detox: The Politics of Disconnecting.* Bingley, UK: Emerald Group Publishing, 2020.

Syvertsen, Trine. *Media Resistance: Protest, Dislike, Abstention.* London: Palgrave Macmillan, 2017.

Syvertsen, Trine, and Gunn Enli. "Digital Detox: Media Resistance and the Promise of Authenticity." *Convergence* 26, no. 5–6 (2020): 1269–83.

Tandoc, Edson C., and Tim P. Vos. "The Journalist Is Marketing the News: Social Media in the Gatekeeping Process." *Journalism Practice* 10, no. 8 (2016): 950–66.

Taylor, Josh. "From 'It's Not a Race' to 'Go for Gold': How Scott Morrison Pivoted on Australia's Covid Vaccine Rollout." *The Guardian Australia*, July 29, 2021. https://www.theguardian.com/society/2021/jul/29/from-its-not-a-race-to-go-for-gold-howscott-morrison-pivoted-on-australias-covid-vaccine-rollout.

Terranova, Tiziana. "Free Labor: Producing Culture for the Digital Economy." *Social Text* 18, no. 2 (June 2000): 33–58.

Tien Vu, Hong. "The Online Audience as Gatekeeper: The Influence of Reader Metrics on News Editorial Selection." *Journalism: Theory, Practice & Criticism* 15, no. 8 (2014): 1094–1110.

Tomasello, Michael. *A Natural History of Human Thinking*. Cambridge, MA: Harvard University Press, 2014.

Tong, Jingrong. "The Defence of Journalistic Legitimacy in Media Discourse in China: An Analysis of the Case of Deng Yujiao." *Journalism* 16, no. 3 (February 2014): 429–46.

Tormoen, Erik. "Champions of Change in Minnesota: Kyndell Harkness." *Minnesota Monthly*, March 5, 2021. https://www.minnesotamonthly.com/lifestyle/champions-of-change-inminnesota-kyndell-harkness/.

Torsner, Sara. "Increasing Numbers of Physical Attacks on European Journalists as They Report on COVID and Other Stories." *The Conversation*, January 6, 2022. https://theconversation.com/increasing-numbers-of-physical-attacks-on-european-journalists as-they-report-on-covid-and-other-stories-173941.

Treem, Jeffrey W., and Paul M. Leonardi. "Social Media Use in Organizations: Exploring the Affordances of Visibility, Editability, Persistence, and Association." *Annals of the International Communication Association* 36, no. 1 (2013): 143–89.

Tufekci, Zeynep. "Grooming, Gossip, Facebook and Myspace: What Can We Learn about These Sites from Those Who Won't Assimilate?" *Information, Communication & Society* 11, no. 4 (June 2008): 544–64.

Vaast, Emmanuelle, and Evgeny Kaganer. "Social Media Affordances and Governance in the Workplace: An Examination of Organizational Policies." *Journal of Computer-Mediated Communication* 19, no. 1 (October 2013): 78–101.

"Vaccine Hesitancy Tracker." The Melbourne Institute, 2020. https://melbourneinstitute.unimelb.edu.au/publications/research-insights/ttpn/vaccination-report.

Valenzuela, Sebastián, Ingrid Bachmann, and Matías Bargsted. "The Personal Is the Political? What Do Whatsapp Users Share and How It Matters for News Knowledge, Polarization and Participation in Chile." *Digital Journalism* 9, no. 2 (2021): 155–75.

Vallas, Steven P., and Angèle Christin. "Work and Identity in an Era of Precarious Employment: How Workers Respond to 'Personal Branding' Discourse." *Work and Occupations* 45, no. 1 (February 2018): 3–37.

Van Bavel, Jay J., Elizabeth A. Harris, Philip Pärnamets, Steve Rathje, Kimberly C. Doell, and Joshua A. Tucker. "Political Psychology in the Digital (Mis) Information Age: A Model of News Belief and Sharing." *Social Issues and Policy Review* 15, no. 1 (2021): 84–113.

Van Dijck, José, Thomas Poell, and Martijn De Waal. *The Platform Society: Public Values in a Connective World*. Oxford: Oxford University Press, 2018.

Van Dijk, Johannes. "Digital Divide Research, Achievements and Shortcomings." *Poetics* 34, no. 4–5 (August 2006): 221–35.

Van Zoonen, Ward, Joost W. M. Verhoeven, and Rens Vliegenthart. "How Employees Use Twitter to Talk about Work: A Typology of Work-Related Tweets." *Computers in Human Behavior* 55 (February 2016): 329–39.

Veum, Aslaug, Moland Undrum, and Linda Victoria. "The Selfie as a Global Discourse." *Discourse and Society* 29, no. 1 (2017): 86–103.

Viljoen, Salomé. "The Promise and Limits of Lawfulness: Inequality, Law, and the Techlash." *Journal of Social Computing* 2, no. 3 (2021): 284–96.

Vu, Hong Tien. "The Online Audience as Gatekeeper: The Influence of Reader Metrics on News Editorial Selection." *Journalism: Theory, Practice & Criticism* 15, no. 8 (November 2014): 1094–1110. https://doi.org/10.1177/1464884913504259.

Waddell, T. Franklin. "What Does the Crowd Think? How Online Comments and Popularity Metrics Affect News Credibility and Issue Importance." *New Media & Society* 20, no. 8 (August 2018): 3068–83.

Waisbord, Silvio. "Mob Censorship: Online Harassment of US Journalists in Times of Digital Hate and Populism." *Digital Journalism* 8, no. 8 (2020): 1030–46.

Walsh, Nonee, Abeer Saady, and Fiona Martin. "Why Do We Have to Search for a Line Here and There on Safety for Women Journalists?" *Australian Journalism Review* 40, no. 2 (2018): 67–71.

Walters, Patrick. "Reclaiming Control: How Journalists Embrace Social Media Logics While Defending Journalistic Values." *Digital Journalism* 10, no. 9 (2021): 1–20. https://doi.org/10.1080/21670811.2021.1942113.

Wang, Dan, Vincent Lei Huang, and Steve Zhongshi Guo. "Malleable Multiplicity and Power Reliance: Identity Presentation by Chinese Journalists on Social Media." *Digital Journalism* 8, no. 10 (2020): 1280–97. https://doi.org/10.1080/21670811.2020.1832900.

Watkins, Jerry, Sora Park, R. Warwick Blood, Michelle Dunne Breen, Glen Fuller, Franco Papandrea, and Matthew Ricketson. "Digital News Report: Australia 2015." News and Media Research Centre, University of Canberra, 2015. https://apo.org.au/node/55257.

"We Belong Here: Pushing Back against Online Harassment." Online News Association, 2015. https://www.youtube.com/watch?v=Jpy0AGLURN8&ab_channel=OnlineNewsAssociation.

Wells, Jamelle. "ABC Journalist Louise Milligan Agrees to Pay MP Andrew Laming $79,000 in Defamation Settlement." *ABC News*, August 10, 2021. https://www.abc.net.au/news/2021-0811/nsw-louise-milligan-to-pay-andrew-laming-in-defamation-case/100367922.

Westlund, Oscar. "Producer-Centric versus Participation-Centric: On the Shaping of Mobile Media." *Northern Lights: Film & Media Studies Yearbook* 10, no. 1 (May 2012): 107–21.

"What's Gone Wrong with Australia's Vaccine Rollout?" *BBC News*, June 17, 2021. https://www.bbc.com/news/world-australia-56825920.

Wihbey, John. Twitter, September 18, 2021. https://twitter.com/wihbey/status/1438921646644121601.

Wihbey, John, Garrett Morrow, Myojung Chung, and Mike Peacey. "The Bipartisan Case for Labeling as a Content Moderation Method: Findings from a National Survey." SSRN, 2021. https://papers.ssrn.com/sol3/papers.cfm?abstract_id=3923905.

Williams, John. "The Basics of Branding." *Entrepreneur*, 2012. http://www.entrepreneur.com/article/77408.

"Workers' Rights." International Federation of Journalists. https://www.ifj.org/what/workers rights.html.

"World Press Trends." World Association of News Publishers, 2021. https://wan-ifra.org/world press-trends.

Xu, Nairui. "Digital Media and Investigative Journalism in China." *Media Asia* 48, no. 3 (2021): 158–74.

Yates, Dean. "Burying Mental Health Stigma and Building Wellness." Thomson Reuters. https://www.thomsonreuters.com/en/careers/careers-blog/burying-mental-health-stigma.html.

Yum, Haiqing. "Beyond Gatekeeping: J-blogging in China." *Journalism* 14, no. 4 (May 2011): 379–93.

Zelizer, Barbie. "Journalists as Interpretive Communities." *Critical Studies in Mass Communication* 10, no. 3 (September 1993): 219–37.

Zhang, Shuling, and Qiong Wang. "Refracting the Pandemic: A Field Theory Approach to Chinese Journalists' Sourcing Options in the Age of COVID-19." *Digital Journalism* 10, no. 6 (2022): 1115–34.

Index

New York Times: Black staff, 61–62; criticism by Tucker Carlson, 93; social media policy, 63, 64, 65, 66
non-risky behavior, 40. *See also* risk management
nonuse, 3, 4, 28, 29, 40, 109
National Public Radio (NPR), 122n5

objectivity, 6, 16, 55, 66, 69
online extremism, 94
online persona. *See* personal online identity
online publics, 11, 20, 34, 114
online spaces, 11, 16, 28, 32, 85; added value of, 4, 35, 37, 40
Online Violence Response Hub, 93
online work practices. *See* labor
openness, 42, 67, 107, 110. *See also* transparency
opinion, 22, 36, 40, 52, 65–66, 73, 85, 86
organizational affiliation, 52, 55, 70, 84
organizational branding. *See* branding
organizational policies. *See* social media guidelines/policies for journalists
organizational routines, 34
Organization for Economic Co-operation and Development (OECD), 77

Panama Papers, 2
paradox, 2–4, 8–9, 16, 29, 45–47, 59–60, 62–63, 69–73, 111
participation. *See* audiences
peer-support networks, 97, 103, 110
people of color, 61–62, 93
performance, 19, 24, 50, 51, 59
personal boundaries: blurring of, 3, 26, 34, 52; establishing, 32–42, 104, 109, 110–11
personal branding, 45–60
personality-based posting. *See* influencers
personal online identity, 17–18, 22–23, 32–34, 36, 37, 38, 40–43, 65, 70, 100, 101. *See also* personal branding
platformization, 46, 113
policy. *See* social media guidelines/policies (for journalists)
political conspiracy, 82, 88, 90, 94
politicization of information, 82, 87, 91
populist politics, 48, 94

positive impacts/outcomes, 7, 27, 28, 108, 114
positive interactions, 67, 72, 100
post-traumatic stress disorder (PTSD), 110. *See also* trauma
Poynter, 96
precarity. *See* labor: precarious
privacy, 27, 33, 40, 64, 67–68, 73, 94, 109, 110
professionalization, 9, 16, 19, 32, 37, 41, 56, 84, 95, 101
protest aesthetic, 83. *See also* antilockdown
protests, 61, 83, 85
provaccination, 83–84
public mistrust, 15, 78, 79. *See also* trust

QAnon, 82
"Queen of Facts," 86–88. *See also* Vella, Sharnelle

racism, 61, 62, 67, 94. *See also* Black Lives Matter
reciprocity, 21, 24–26, 59
regulation of markets, 28, 48, 49, 64, 104–5
repetition of information, 79
reputation: building of, 37, 47, 49, 50, 53, 55, 89; damage of, 9, 17, 33, 36, 37, 55, 58, 95; management of, 35, 49, 50, 56, 59, 64–67, 73, 96. *See also* defamation; risk management
Reuters, 3, 97, 103, 109–10
Ressa, Maria, 1
risk management, 33, 34, 36, 40, 55, 56, 57, 58, 63, 65–67, 70, 71, 73, 92, 96, 102, 103, 113
rules of engagement, 38–39, 56, 98
rural news, 22, 31–32

self-care, 97
self-censorship, 33, 36, 37, 100
self-disclosure, 65, 69
self-promotion, 10, 80, 87
self-representation, 19, 37, 41, 46, 85
shadow banned, 84
social authority, 6, 78
social behaviors, 19, 21, 42, 82
social capital, 18. *See also* personal branding
social expectations, 33, 95, 108

DIANA BOSSIO is an associate professor in media and communication at Swinburne University and the author of *Journalism and Social Media: Practitioners, Organisations, and Institutions* and coeditor of *Social Media and the Politics of Reportage: The Arab Spring*.

VALÉRIE BÉLAIR-GAGNON is an associate professor and Cowles fellow in media management at the University of Minnesota, Twin Cities, and the author of *Social Media at BBC News* and coauthor of *Journalism Research that Matters* and coauthor of *Happiness in Journalism*.

AVERY E. HOLTON is an associate professor and department chair in the Department of Communication at the University of Utah and coauthor of *Happiness in Journalism*.

LOGAN MOLYNEUX is an associate professor of journalism at Temple University.

The University of Illinois Press
is a founding member of the
Association of University Presses.

———————————

University of Illinois Press
1325 South Oak Street
Champaign, IL 61820-6903
www.press.uillinois.edu